GETTING ME

The Secret To
What Your Spouse Really Wants

Gregg Medlyn & Candace Winslow

© Medlyn & Winslow, LLC

Print ISBN: 978-1-48359-182-7

eBook ISBN: 978-1-48359-183-4

To Ruth

Thank you for always being so loving, kind and supportive — especially throughout the writing of this book. I could not have done it without you!

To John

For the days behind and the days ahead, know I always think of you.

To Caroline and Grant

May the Lord bless you as amply as He did your mom in the gift of a spouse.
I love you all more than written words could ever express.

Contents

Finding the Courage to Save My Marriage 3

By Candace Winslow

What Happens in Gregg's Office? 11

By Gregg Medlyn

Conversation 1 — **Intentional Date Night** 27

Conversation 2 — **Comings and Goings** 46

Conversation 3 — **Couch Time** 63

Conversation 4 — **State of the Union** 85

Conversation 5 — **Pillow Talk** 98

Conversation 6 — **Sacred Time** 114

Be the Twenty Percent 133

By Gregg Medlyn

Acknowledgements

Three years ago we set out on a journey with only a vision of the book you now hold in your hands. Little did we know how exhilarating, challenging, and at times, exhausting the process of writing this book would be! And yet like most worthy things in life, we did not accomplish this task alone. We were incredibly blessed to have a few key people come alongside us to offer their help along the way.

From the very beginning, the encouragement and coaching from *Jeff Morton* and *Matt Jacob* helped launch our writing process. Jeff's assuredness that we could construct content that would make a difference in marriages was foundational to our start. Matt's expertise and experience helped with our further understanding of good writing, and served as a terrific source of encouragement.

Our officemate and graphic designer, *Bobby Friske*, was paramount in helping us express our thoughts in pictures. Many times, he asked just the right question to help us not only articulate our words more effectively, but also visualize the accompanying picture to the words. Bobby was the first person to suggest that we (Gregg and Candace) made for great working partners. And Bobby, like no other, made us laugh along the way.

God, in His great attention to detail, gave us *Karen Katulka* at the last phase of writing for a complete edit of our manuscript. Karen proved to be so much more than our editor: she was our cheerleader, our comforter, our minister, our enthusiasm, and she was our friend with every step of reading and re-reading the words in these pages. She believed in our work when, at times, we could not.

And finally, we acknowledge our families as our cornerstones. I (Gregg) thank my wife, *Ruth*, for her continued love, encouragement and patience through this journey. I also thank my dog, *Molly*, for her unconditional love and faithfulness as my canine companion. I (Candace) thank my children, *Caroline* and *Grant*, for their understanding and patience when they often found their mom behind closed study doors working on this book. And I also thank my husband, *John*, who so often sees more in me than I do in myself.

Our prayer is that God will bless your reading of this book. May He show you one new concept, one sentence or one phrase that will ultimately draw you closer to Him and to each other. May our work and this book be for His glory and His alone!

Finding the Courage to Save My Marriage

by Candace Winslow

On October 15, 1994, I walked down the aisle toward the love of my life, filled with nothing but hope and confidence that ours would be the model marriage. We were two people who could withstand any hardship, rise up over any obstacle. No one in the world *got* me the way John *got* me. What could possibly rattle our marriage? Absolutely nothing, I thought.

Those of you who have been married more than two weeks are already chuckling at my naiveté. Even though I felt "maritally invincible" on my wedding day, I soon realized that a great marriage does not happen by chance nor can it be sustained by overwhelming confidence. A great marriage is the result of a lot of intentionality, a lot of communication, and a lot of work.

To begin my story, you must know I married a man who is the definition of selfless. He inherited from his mother an unbelievable ability to put other people first. In the first years of our marriage, he would always say to me, "I just want you to be happy." I never could believe him. It sounded like something he thought he was supposed to say as a husband.

The reason why I couldn't believe him was mainly because I am so different from John. John married a woman who is the definition of selfish. I tend to think of *myself* first, want to accomplish *my* agenda first, and want *my* voice to be heard first.

It's hard to write those words but I share them to say that even when "selfish" marries "selfless," a healthy marriage is possible. However, it's only possible if the desire to work on the marriage exists each and every day. John and I celebrated 22 years of marriage this year, so we are living proof. But it has not always been this way.

A Valley of Disconnection

About five years into our marriage, John and I hit rock bottom. We were both miserable in our relationship. We got to this place for one reason and one reason only: terrible communication. There was no outside trigger that took us to the valley of disconnection — no affair, no addiction, no life circumstance. We just stopped communicating. We were talking to each other, but we were not communicating. I suddenly became overwhelmed by the thought that John did not *get* me anymore — and this scared me.

On our lowest day, I told John that I did not love him. I told him I would stay in our marriage only because I had vowed to God in front of 200 people that I would. But in staying, I quickly added, I knew I would be miserable for the rest of my life. I have played that scene from 1997 in my mind over and over and even now, 19 years later, the words bring painful tears to my eyes.

After angrily saying those words to John, I walked around the corner to our staircase, sat down and prayed, "God, I am so angry. You have to help me." It took everything within me to pray those words because

I really just wanted to leave. Nothing immediately changed after the prayer. But it was the first step toward our journey of healing and the investment that has made our marriage what it is today.

At this point of crisis in our marriage, John and I were blessed to work with a wonderful marriage therapist (second to Gregg, of course!) who recognized that we were two different people, with two different temperaments and two different sets of expectations unsuccessfully trying to merge together as "one flesh." Even though our early years of dating led both of us to believe that we *got* one another, it became abundantly clear we did not. But, because our ultimate goal was to *get* one another, our therapist helped us learn how to communicate. We were in therapy over 15 years ago, and the return on that investment has paid off year after year in our marriage.

As a minister, I have used my personal experience to help other married women and have seen time and time again that often what tears a marriage apart starts with communication. It seems like communication should be the easiest thing to "fix," but I know from firsthand experience and walking alongside others that this is not true. Communication is so incredibly complex — yet so incredibly important for a healthy marriage. And what you will find in the pages of this book is that healthy communication is key to *getting* your spouse.

It turns out that communication is about far more than just words. It's body language; it's nonverbal responses. It's deep sighs and rolling of the eyes; it's indifference when your spouse shares something that is important to him or her. Whether or not I use words, I communicate with John in one way or another all day long. And it's in these moments that I have learned how vital healthy communication is in a marriage. So vital, learning how to have healthy communication saves marriages just like mine. And just like yours.

A Bond to Break Down the Barriers

Which brings me to my partnership with Gregg Medlyn. When I first met Gregg, my ministry was centered on working with women who were in abusive relationships. I introduced myself to Gregg, not for how I could help him, but for how he could help me better minister to women who were suffering with pain from abuse. That simple introduction was the seed of an almost 10-year friendship.

What also surfaced from our meetings was our shared passion for good communication in marriage. I heard Gregg say nearly every time we met that the primary reason couples needed marital counseling was to develop healthier communication. I resonated with this because it was exactly what took me and John to counseling when we hit rock bottom. I can testify that good communication saved my marriage! For Gregg, he learned this lesson through a different process of re-marriage — but it's a lesson he and his wife apply daily to their own thriving relationship.

We agreed that blending Gregg's marriage therapy background with my theological background could help couples learn how to better communicate in order to *get* one another. Our partnership in writing this book is a shared commitment to making a difference in how husbands and wives communicate and to help break down the barriers standing between so many.

What makes us unique as authors is the nature of our partnership:

- We are both married, but not to each other.
- One of us is in a first marriage, the other is divorced and re-married.
- One of us has two kids, the other has no kids — but the world's best dog!

- One of us is a licensed marriage and family therapist, the other a degreed seminarian.

What bonds us is a collective passion to help married couples establish and sustain a healthy, holy marriage. We believe each couple that engages in continuous *Getting Me* conversations will experience a powerful sense of connection — physically, emotionally, and spiritually — far greater than their marriage has ever experienced before.

Which Marriages Last?

Gregg has counseled hundreds and hundreds of married couples in his practice as a licensed marriage and family therapist. Based on his experience and observations, he knows that of the married couples who come into his office seeking counsel:

- 20% of the couples will divorce
- 60% of the couples will stay married, but will make little or no improvements in their marriage
- 20% of the couples will change their habits, their behavior, and their thinking in order to improve and strengthen their marriage.

In other words, only 2 out of 10 couples work to improve their marriage. Those are not very attractive odds! But if you can look past the daunting outlook of those numbers, surely the first question in your mind is: what separates the 20 percent from the 80 percent?

Only 2 out of 10 couples will have the courage to evaluate all aspects of their marriage and commit to each other to take action. Only 2 out of 10 couples will view their marriage as their most important relationship — more important than relationships with their kids, parents, colleagues or friends — and will commit to intentionally focusing on developing the best marriage possible.

Think about it. Improving your marriage is no different than improving your health and fitness. You already know what needs to be done to lose weight: take in fewer calories than you

> *Only 2 out of 10 couples will have the courage to evaluate all aspects of their marriage and commit to each other to take action.*

expend each day. You already know what it takes to have a physically fit body: exercise 3-5 times a week for 30 minutes or more. Understanding how to live a healthy lifestyle or how to be physically fit is the simple part. What makes sustaining a healthy and fit lifestyle challenging is actually doing the work of eating healthy and exercising regularly. Health and fitness is that simple yet it requires hard work and commitment.

Most couples fall in the 80 percent category because they do not look at their marriage intentionally. At some point, between six months to two years after their wedding day, married couples slide into a comfort zone. Spouses forget their manners with each other. The person who should be their greatest cheerleader somehow becomes their greatest challenge. Spouses start acting as though the purpose of their marriage is to have their individual needs met, rather than meeting the needs of their spouse first.

And what's worse, married couples will spend very limited, if any, time or resources to make their marriage better. Compare your marriage to the time, money, and effort you have spent devoted to your favorite hobby. If you are a golfer, how much money on golf lessons and new clubs — or how much time at the driving range — have you spent in the last year improving your game? If you are into fashion, how many fashion magazines do you subscribe to, how much shopping have you done looking for the latest trend, and how much time do you spend planning your wardrobe to look your best? Just as you pursue your hobby with time, money and effort, we contend you must pursue developing and sustaining your marriage in the same way.

Will *You* Have the Courage to Save *Your* Marriage?

Gregg and I are looking for the 2 couples out of 10 who really want to have a healthy relationship. We want to connect through the pages of this book with those couples who are willing to invest the time, the effort, the mental space, the money, and the courage to make their marriage stronger. You will know you are one of the committed couples if your desire to change is greater than your willingness to live with any hardship you are experiencing in your marriage.

We come to this work with a Christian worldview, which will be prevalent in the coming pages. We both affirm that Christ is not only the chief cornerstone of a healthy marriage, but for every individual in all aspects of life. However, regardless of your faith orientation, we believe these principles are applicable to all married couples, from the newlywed still unpacking from the honeymoon to the couple celebrating 50 years.

Don't Give Up

I didn't realize it at the time, but John and I are one of the two couples who were willing to do the hard work to save our marriage. After six months of marriage therapy, we were able to begin healing what had been terribly broken between us. When we both had the courage to admit we couldn't do it on our own anymore, and started working together to learn how to communicate better, our marriage started to heal. We started to *get* one another again —now in new and wonderful ways.

And by God's grace, at that same time of healing, we discovered we both had a shared interest in running a marathon. So, we started training together. It was in those painful hours and hours (and hours!) of training and working together toward the common goal of crossing the finish line that we found victory.

You and your spouse may be at mile one of your marathon — so to speak — full of energy to take on any problem that may come your way. Or you may be at mile 15, where the end of the race seems nowhere in sight and quitting has crossed your mind. I want to urge you to keep running together. My prayer is that, like me and John as we crossed the finish line of the New York City marathon, you and your spouse will finish this race together and be overwhelmed by joy as you do.

What Happens in Gregg's Office?

by Gregg Medlyn

When Laura* and Andy* came into my office I knew things weren't good. Andy entered with eyes that screamed, "Help!" as he sat down on the couch. Laura's arms were crossed tightly as she entered behind him and sat down as far away as possible from her husband. Their tension was so thick it made my office feel uncomfortably tight. I sat down and asked, "What is your hope for coming to see me today?"

Laura could hardly speak, but coldly expressed, "He ruined our marriage." Andy took a deep breath and began his defense. "Gregg, she hasn't slept with me since Morgan was born — and that was 8 months ago! What was I supposed to do? She clearly doesn't *get* that I need sex."

Through gritted teeth, Laura scoffed, "So, he slept with his co-worker. While I was home nursing OUR child, cooking OUR dinner, cleaning OUR home. He clearly doesn't *get me* and why I'm completely exhausted when he comes prancing in ready for sex."

Laura and Andy stared at me with anger and fear in their eyes. I had seen these expressions countless times before. Every couple, regardless of the details of their circumstances, enters my office because they are in some kind of marital pain. They come because the pain of their marriage staying the same has become greater than the pain of changing.

Why Marriages *Really* Struggle

As a solution-focused therapist, I begin every first session with the question, "What is your hope for coming to see me today?" because I want the couple to start envisioning what their marriage could be as a result of counseling. Some of the more common answers I hear are:

"She's too tired to have sex with me."

"He doesn't help with the kids."

"She doesn't appreciate me for all the hard work I do to provide."

"He won't stop looking at pornography. Am I not good enough?"

"She micromanages me all day every day."

Their responses, though honest, don't answer my question. Most often, couples answer with what or who is causing the pain. Their focus is on what they *don't* want or *don't* do well versus what they *do* want or *do* do well.

Regardless of what happened or who's to blame, one answer I hear most consistently from every couple is:

"Our communication is horrible."

When a couple tells me they don't communicate well, I affirm that they actually *are* communicating well! Nonverbals alone can communicate more than enough. You can tell when your wife is angry, can't you? You can tell when your husband is ready for sex without him having to say a word, right? Your body language, a certain look, or turning away and rolling your eyes — it's all communication. Communication is more than talking.

Why is communication so important? What is it about communication with your spouse that makes or breaks your marriage, or your long-awaited dinner date, or what should be a peaceful time once the kids are finally tucked into bed? Why do the words your wife or husband says to you on a daily basis — or doesn't say — contribute so strongly to the bottom line of your marriage? Why does poor communication lead to so many fights?

Good, intentional conversation is the key to *getting* your spouse. It's the only way to grow in the discovery of and intimacy with the person whom you vowed to spend the rest of your life. When you and your spouse are effectively communicating, you are listening and observing, while talking and sharing. Effective communication — both verbal and nonverbal — should help you both understand one another better.

It's when we aren't communicating in a healthy way that fights surface. And this unhealthy way of communicating is where most marital conflicts begin.

What You Are Really Fighting About

I tell all of my clients that God has given humans four primary feelings: mad, sad, glad and fear. Though you may immediately debate that fact by listing many more, I contend these four feelings are from where every emotion stems. These four primary feelings are universal to mankind and "mix" together to give us a myriad of emotions — just like primary colors blend together to produce an endless spectrum of hues. For example, the feeling you call "frustrated," is actually a mix of feeling both mad and fearful about the circumstance you have found yourself in. Or what you call "disappointed," is actually sadness mixed with underlying fear. Once you understand that you have these four primary feelings — mad, sad, glad, and fear — you can begin to decipher the emotional responses you experience.

Having this knowledge is paramount to understanding what you are really fighting about as a couple. Let's look at a specific example of arguing about sex in your marriage to illustrate this point.

ON THE SURFACE

ON THE SURFACE	What you fight about: • Sex, money, the dog, work, where to eat, fill in the blank • Feelings of anger

On the surface, your fight looks like it is about your lack of sex. You and your spouse cross another night off the calendar having had no sexual intimacy whatsoever. Your husband makes a snide comment about not being able to count on you. Your wife gets defensive that she's overworked and underappreciated in the home. And just like that, the fight begins.

But what is really going on?

BELOW THE SURFACE

BELOW THE SURFACE	On a deeper level, you fight about: • Not feeling loved, appreciated, respected • Feelings of sadness

If you dig a little deeper, what you are *really* fighting about is far from your lack of sex (or where to eat, or over-spending, or a lack of quality time together). On the surface it may seem you're fighting because you're angry, but below the surface, the fight evolves from sadness that you don't feel loved, appreciated or respected. Husbands, doesn't she know you've worked hard this week and you simply want to connect with her? It *is* sad that the woman you love the most doesn't want to have sex with you.

AT THE CORE

AT THE CORE	What you really fight about: • Not feeling heard, understood, known • Feelings of fear

This below-the-surface cause for fighting is a long-held belief by most therapists. But I believe we can pinpoint the cause for fighting even more precisely. At the core of every fight is <u>fear</u>. You fear that your spouse doesn't hear, understand or know you.

So wives, why doesn't he *get* that you don't want to have sex because you've been tugged and pulled at all day by your children, and that being touched again is the last thing you want? If he *got* you, he wouldn't put you in a position where you had to reject him. So the presenting fight is about a lack of sex, but the true, underlying issue is your belief that your spouse doesn't hear, understand or know you. Your fear is that your spouse doesn't *get* you — and that he or she never will.

Let's look at this as a complete visual.

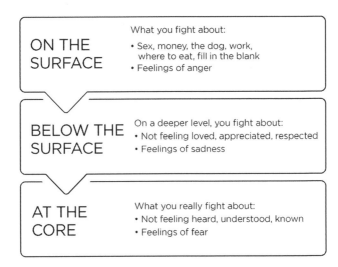

Who *Gets* You?

On your wedding day, you placed a wedding band on the one person who you believed actually *got* you. You stood at the altar and saw the only person who knew you inside and out. This person was the one person on earth who understood you more profoundly than anyone else. Then sometime between the wedding night and six months into the marriage, you started seeing signs that your spouse didn't actually *get* every part of you. Your husband kept saying he'd change the front porch light bulb (which you consider a safety issue), but he never got around to it. Your wife stopped wearing lingerie to bed, and started going to bed earlier and without you. Eventually you started questioning if you are even still married to the same person who pursued you wholeheartedly in dating.

Fast forward to today, you've wondered if your spouse even *wants* to *get* you anymore?

What is *Getting Me*?

Getting Me is a series of six essential conversations that share one goal: to *hear*, *understand*, and *know* your spouse.

As spouses spend time communicating with the objective to understand and to know each other, the outcome is that they feel loved, appreciated and respected, even if they don't agree on the topic at hand.

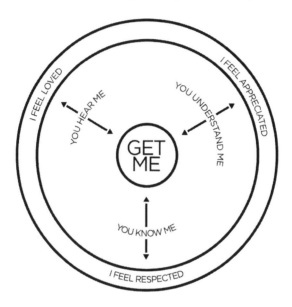

Let's look at an example to demonstrate the point. Say in a marriage the wife loves sushi, while the husband hates sushi. Because of this difference, the couple never goes out to her favorite restaurant on date nights because the husband feels so strongly against raw fish. What happens in this situation? The wife feels her husband minimizes her desire for sushi and that ultimately, her needs are not as important as his. Over time, a simple issue like food preferences can build up marital resentment.

The premise of Getting Me suggests that when differences occur in marriage, the goal is to communicate in a way that allows each spouse to know and understand why the other thinks and feels the way they do.

So back to the example. If the husband listens with the purpose of knowing and understanding why his wife loves sushi instead of making his case that sushi is terrible, he may find that what his wife really likes is simply fresh seafood. So, once discovering this fact, then the conversation can open up to other possibilities for dining options, like a great steakhouse that serves fresh seafood. Another possible solution is to visit the sushi restaurant and the husband order California rolls. By listening with the goal to understand his wife, the husband demonstrates his desire to know why she feels the way she does and in turn, she feels respected and appreciated by the fact that he wants to learn more.

We use a silly example here to prove a bigger point. Getting Me is a continual emphasis, through six essential conversations, that help spouses communicate in such a way to hear, to understand and to know each other. And as each spouse presses into this concept, the result is that the spouse feels loved, appreciated and respected.

Again, the goal of *Getting Me* is not to agree with your spouse's point of view, or to change your spouse's point of view, but to hear, understand and know your spouse. When you engage in *Getting Me* conversations, your goal is to listen in such a way to understand why your spouse feels, thinks and believes the way he or she does. You temporarily suspend your own opinions and needs and begin to "play detective" for the sake of understanding.

> *The goal of **Getting Me** is not to agree with your spouse's point of view, or to change your spouse's point of view, but to hear, understand and know your spouse.*

If you are a parent, you already know this type of listening. When your toddler says, "I don't feel well," you ask questions to figure out exactly how they are hurting, what might have caused the hurt, and what the next step of care should be for your child. You suspend your own perceived opinion of his situation, to decipher what your child is trying to communicate to you.

In the same way, if you are committed to *getting* your spouse, you are so focused on listening to understand that you are deciphering their words to determine their meaning. You suspend your own analysis, and allow your spouse the opportunity to tell you what it is he or she wants you to know.

Why Your Spouse Doesn't Get You

What typically happens when we start out from two different viewpoints or beliefs? Don't we try to prove the other person wrong for their flawed opinion? Wouldn't he be better off if he thought just like you? This way of thinking causes conflict to erupt. Mean, hurtful, or degrading words are often spewed and couples walk away from these types of disagreements feeling deflated and defeated.

Apply this to the topic of spending. Countless couples present to me a similar issue where one or both individuals feel entitled to spending money his or her own way. I hear so often from the husband, "If she *got* me she wouldn't criticize me for spending money on golf clubs!" And from the wife I hear, "If he *got* me he wouldn't question how much I spend, since he doesn't understand how much it takes to run a household."

A more provocative example is when a couple is in my office because of an affair. What I always hear from the spouse that <u>had</u> the affair is, "My spouse doesn't *get* me, but [this other person] does."

There are several different triggers for feeling like your spouse doesn't *get* you. The more common ones are:

- Having the same fight over and over
- Not engaging in conversation
- Lack of taking action around the house
- No eye contact, too focused on work or phone
- Over-promise/under-deliver (she didn't do what she said she would do)
- Feeling not on the same page
- Responding defensively
- Excessive arguing
- Minimizing thoughts and/or feelings
- Not feeling prioritized
- Not spending time together

The most common reactions to feeling like your spouse doesn't *get* you are:

- Anger
- Raising voices
- Starting a fight
- Escalating emotions
- Shaming
- Name-calling
- Shutting down
- Walking away

Couples often think that *getting* one another means they have to *agree* with one another. This isn't true. The goal is to understand the way your spouse thinks, feels, and what it is that he or she wants. You will know you *get* your spouse when you can honestly say — regardless if you agree or not — "I *get* why you [feel/think/believe] that way!" I urge my clients to strive to *get* their spouse.

The Six Essential *Getting Me* Conversations

At the core of every fight or issue in your marriage is the fear that your spouse doesn't *get* you. So, how do you get your spouse to *get* you? It's a romantic idea that your spouse should be able to read your mind, but since telepathy hasn't worked well thus far, you must use your words. And it's how you use your words, what words you use, and how often you share your thoughts, feelings and needs that will help your spouse understand who you are. As you change and grow, taking part in *Getting Me* conversations with your spouse is one of the only ways to ensure you keep discovering who he or she is.

This book demonstrates how to *get* your spouse through a series of six essential conversations that will teach you and your spouse how to communicate in peaceful times (Intentional Date Night), in the everyday activities (Comings and Goings), in conflict (Couch Time), in goal-setting (State of the Union), when you want intimate emotional connection (Pillow Talk), and in sacred moments (Sacred Time).

> *You [God] made the delicate, inner parts of my body and knit me together in my mother's womb. Thank you for making me so wonderfully complex!*
>
> *Psalm 139:13-14a (NLT)*

21

Candace and I want you to realize that your spouse is an ever-growing, changing and beautiful creation from God. Your husband is not one-dimensional. Your wife is not too complicated. You are both human. Psalm 139 reminds us that we were all created by a loving God who used a generous amount of creativity and complexity in His design of each one of us. There is much to be discovered about your spouse. The opportunities to *get* your spouse are endless.

Your husband is not who he was when you first married. Your wife's preferences have changed since you had kids. These changes are not to be cause for concern, but an encouraging sign that your spouse is constantly changing and growing. But you can only understand who your spouse is today by making time for communication.

Will *Getting Me* Conversations Save Our Marriage?

Is healthy communication the cure for your stagnant/neutral/deteriorating (you fill in the blank) marriage? We think so.

"How many times do I have to tell you?" Have you ever said that before in a heated argument with your spouse? Our human nature is not to change the way we explain ourselves to one another — but to talk louder and over our spouse. (Maybe if I scream like a child, my husband will hear me! Probably not.) We wrote *Getting Me* to help you share with one another who you are today. These conversations are meant to create intimacy, not angst.

You may be wounded as you enter into these conversations. Since you were married, one or both of you have likely been hurt by the other. This can cause some pause in wanting to get started, especially if you have lost some trust within your marriage or are fearful of conflict (which will likely arise!). But if you are interested in enriching your marriage, then you are in the 20 percent who are willing to do the hard work. And we are excited to see how these conversations will help you and your spouse feel more loved, appreciated and respected.

The Absence of Four Things and the Presence of Two

 If there are major relationship issues like abuse, adultery, addiction and mental illness present in your marriage, you must address these issues first. There is no *Getting Me* conversation that will solve issues connected to physical, emotional or verbal abuse. If your spouse is still in an active affair, he or she must end it before you begin the process of healing and *getting* one another. If you have found yourselves in any of these circumstances, we highly recommend you seek the help of a professional and have referral sources for help listed at www.getting-me.com.

I tell every couple that comes in my office that only if they are addressing active abuse, addiction, adultery and mental illness can we begin work. And the presence of only two things is what will make it successful: 1) the willingness to do the work — and then the hard part, 2) actually doing the work.

Before You Begin the Book

Before you begin the book, we want you to assess your marriage using the following questions. Your answers are simply <u>your</u> answers, not what you think as a couple, but rather what you think as a partner in the marriage.

- How much time do we spend monthly discovering something new about each other?

- How much conflict are we experiencing in our marriage and how quickly can we resolve it?

- How much time and money do we invest in collective goals for our marriage?

- How secure do I feel in our marriage?

- How much do I serve my spouse in our marriage?

- How connected do I feel to my spouse emotionally?

- How connected do I feel to my spouse physically?

We highly recommend you record your answers in a journal to serve as a starting point for later reference after you have read through and interacted with the *Getting Me* conversations. As a result of pursuing your spouse through our six conversations — your answers should be positively different by the end of the book!

How to Read This Book

Unlike a novel that you might read in solitude, we hope you will interact with this book a bit differently. While we hope you enjoy the content and find it easy to read, it's only in the action you take that will help you experience this book most deeply. To maximize your reading experience, this is our suggested way to read *Getting Me*.

- **Buy two copies.** We recommend you and your spouse have your own copy. This allows you to read individually, take notes, highlight the pages, and interact with the text. While it is possible to begin the work of *getting* your spouse on your own, we highly recommend you go through the content together.

- **Order of conversations.** The conversations are listed numerically; however, you do not have to master one conversation before moving on to the next. The order in which we printed the conversations is our suggested order. However, do feel free to start with the conversation that appeals to you most.

- **Start a journal.** Reflection questions are provided to meditate on at the conclusion of each chapter. The journal serves as your personal space to record your answers and write your thoughts about each chapter.

- **Follow the icons.** Each chapter offers three icons that will help guide you through the chapter.

This icon guides you to our website www.getting-me. com. Here you will find a "Reader's Section" with podcasts, blogs, videocasts and more content that will help amplify the book. Be sure to bookmark the website on your computer for easy accessibility.

This icon guides you through the Next Steps you can take to put each *Getting Me* conversation into action immediately.

This icon guides you through Reflection Questions you can answer with your spouse to help you reflect on the content of each Getting Me conversation.

- **Read it as yourself.** Since this book has been written directly to both men and women, we alternate the use of "he" and "she" throughout the entire book. For the sake of simplicity, read it as yourself, and use the pronoun that best suits you.

How Do You Know You Get Your Spouse?

You'll know you've hit "communication bull's-eye" when your spouse feels heard, understood and known. When your spouse asks, "Do you *get* where I'm coming from?" — you can honestly answer *yes*.

At the point when you can answer *yes*, you two will experience a deeper emotional, spiritual and physical connection.

On your wedding day, you knew your marriage was your priority. Keeping it a priority — whether you've been married one year or fifty — requires intentional, open-minded communication. Let's explore how *Getting Me* can help keep your marriage your priority by allowing these conversations to examine and strengthen your marriage so it can be healthy for the years to come.

* Laura and Andy are fictitious characters whose situation represents a common issue present in Gregg's office.

Intentional Date Night

*A*fter a long week of managing children, work demands, and multiple loads of laundry, Tom and Cindy handed off their crying 6-year-old and fussy baby to the beloved babysitter. They backed out of the garage quickly before giving the babysitter a chance to change her mind.

Their monthly date night had finally arrived, and boy did they need it!

Driving away from the house, Tom asked Cindy, "Where do you want to go?" Feeling slightly irritated Tom didn't have a plan, Cindy replied, "I don't know. Where do you want to go?"

Two minutes of back-and-forth indecisiveness landed them at an old standby — a local chain restaurant — not because they were excited to eat there, but because they couldn't think of any place better. Tom parked the car as Cindy's mind swirled with frustration, wishing they could remember the names of the new restaurants they had once said they wanted to try.

After ordering their food, the conversation centered on the usual: work, kids, money, and home. Although they had been waiting all month *for this rare night out, both were surprised that — after 45 minutes in the booth together — they had little left to discuss.*

Tom pulled out his phone to check his work email; Cindy sat irritated, but said nothing. Instead, she posted a picture of their table on Instagram with the caption: "We love date night!"

After a meal full of forced conversation, the check came. Tom suggested a movie as a way to extend the evening, but Cindy said she was too tired.

They went home, paid the babysitter and realized another date night had come and gone, completely void of connection. What started out as a night both looked forward to ended in great disappointment. Again.

Can you relate to Tom and Cindy?

Most books about marriage will suggest "date night" is mandatory in a healthy marriage — and we agree 100 percent. Yet what most marital books or marriage therapists don't tell you is <u>how</u> to date once you're married. Lacking that knowledge cripples couples and keeps them disconnected.

Why Do We Date Anyway?

Think back to the beginning of your relationship. Initially, it was all about going on that first date. With a stomach full of butterflies, you were hopeful that there would be another date, and then another one.

Sure, you were attracted to each other and looked forward to fun outings together. But the real motivating factor for dating was to discover who the other person was and what the other person was all about.

For most couples, those first dates were filled with questions and conversations about each other's family and personal history, a curiosity about what occupied your daily lives and endless discussions about hopes and dreams for the future. Chances are, what made you more attracted to each other was the compelling nature of those answers, something unlike you had experienced on past dates with other people.

On those initial date nights, there was no talk of paying bills, leaving jobs or nagging about being late. You wanted to get to know the other person, all the while making your own best impression. The only things that mattered: what you wore, where you went and how you looked. Do you remember smiling throughout dinner hoping broccoli wasn't stuck in your teeth? These minor concerns are what made that time of dating so precious.

Now, fast forward to your marriage today. Sadly, dates for married couples often follow a less inspiring script. Couples use their date night time to address the inner workings of their marriage — such as finances or home projects. The conversation centers on their kids or issues within the marriage. On the worst date nights, there's no conversation at all. Instead of wanting to discover something new about your spouse, date nights have become just a break in the day-to-day routine.

The date night, in other words, has been hijacked. What was once used for a time of mutual enjoyment, has become a way to get away from the norm of home or work. The date night has become merely a time where you sit across from your spouse showing more interest in your smartphone than in the person in front of you — who incidentally is the same person you once couldn't wait to get to know. The process of *getting* your spouse begins when conversation is intentional and focused on the other person, and often results in experiencing a greater level of intimacy.

Maybe your date nights aren't as stark as we've described. If so, congratulations! Regardless of where your dating life as a married couple falls on the spectrum, we propose adding a fresh perspective: simply add the word *intentional* to this all-too-familiar term "date night."

What is Intentional Date Night?

Intentional Date Night is a dedicated time to go on a date with your spouse with the specific purpose of connecting through the art of discovery. Through the art of discovery, your goal is to get to know and understand at least one new thing about your spouse during your date. Intentional Date Night is intentional in every aspect, from how you plan the date, to how you enjoy the date, to how you end the date.

> *Intentional Date Night is a dedicated time to go on a date with your spouse with the specific purpose of connecting through the art of discovery.*

Married couples often lose track of the need for continual discovery after the initial wedded bliss has worn off. Too many couples stop trying to learn new aspects of their spouse. The healthiest marriages are ones where both people remember their spouse is a God-given gift who has many extraordinary dimensions of character. Remembering this truth about your spouse is especially hard when the day-to-day struggles get in the way. However, Intentional Date Night is a creative and purposeful way for you to break out of your normal daily routine and embrace an opportunity to *get* your spouse.

We want to improve your dating life as a married couple by changing the paradigm of the typical date night issues of where to go, what to do and what to talk about. We want to help you avoid the fights that often happen before the date even begins because expectations for the night aren't met. And most of all, we want to ignite the spark of continual discovery between you and your spouse so that you will experience a greater return from the evening that will last well beyond the date night. After an Intentional Date Night, you will *get* your spouse in at least one new way. This, in turn, will allow him to feel loved, appreciated and respected by you, which will ultimately result in a deeper connection for you both.

How to Plan an Intentional Date Night

So, how *do* you have an Intentional Date Night? The process is divided into five steps:

STEPS TO INTENTIONAL DATE NIGHT

1. Determine who hosts the Intentional Date Night and the specific time for the date.
2. Prepare for Intentional Date Night by using your spouse's Date Night Menu.
3. Ask your spouse on Intentional Date Night.
4. Engage in meaningful conversation during Intentional Date Night.
5. Close your Intentional Date Night.

Step 1: Determine Who Hosts Intentional Date Night and Set the Specific Time for the Date

The great news is Step 1 could not be easier: simply pick a "host" — the planner and organizer for the evening. You and your spouse will alternate host responsibilities between each date. In other words, you will host a date and then your spouse will host the next date, and so forth and so on.

Once the host is determined, the next step is to talk to your spouse to confirm the day and the time of the date. Since there will be planning involved, the host needs a specific day and time. Having this conversation is not the official "ask", this is for logistical planning purposes only. If arrangements for a babysitter need to be made, the host takes on that responsibility. If the host doesn't know the babysitter's contact information, rather than give your spouse the task of lining up child care, refer to the Intentional Date Night Menu (see step 2) and confirm you have the correct information. Remember, the host takes care of all planning elements of the date.

With the host determined and the day and time pinpointed, you are ready to plan the date!

Step 2: Prepare for Intentional Date Night by Using Your Spouse's Intentional Date Night Menu

"Typical" date nights often run the risk of ending in a disagreement because the couple has not planned in advance for their time together. With one person designated as host, you have resolved the "Where do you want to go?" conversation that begins too many dates for married couples.

If you're hosting, remember this: the date is not about what you want, but about what your spouse wants. In other words, if you are planning for Intentional Date Night, the night is designed with your spouse in mind. Why? It's all about *getting* your spouse in a new and deeper way.

As the host of the date, you want to plan a time where you are creating not only an enjoyable date, but also an environment where you both can quickly connect at a deeper level through intentional conversation. Husbands, for this example, let's say you're the one planning the date. By demonstrating to your wife that you're capable of putting her interests above your own, you're creating a time where she can see in full effect your ability to love and respect her.

WWW To eliminate any planning obstacles, we have created the Intentional Date Night Menu, which is also found on our website: www.getting-me.com. To explain the concept of Intentional Date Night, here is an example of an Intentional Date Night Menu:

INTENTIONAL DATE NIGHT MENU

Name: Cindy   As of: April 17, 2017

● **RESTAURANTS I LIKE TO VISIT**

1. Sandy's Cafe on Hall Street
2. Borderline on Smith Street
3. Jones Steak House on Pomona Avenue
4. Café Thomas on Forest Lane
5. Harry's on Fondren Road
6. Sam's BBQ on Jones Avenue

● **PLACES I LIKE TO GO (NO TIME RESTRAINT)**

1. Contemporary Art Museum
2. Southland Park when the weather is nice
3. Farmers' Market
4. Westside Shopping Mall
5. Walk around any lakes in our city
6. Observation deck in the Tower Building downtown

● **THINGS I LIKE TO DO (REQUIRES A SPECIFIC TIME FRAME)**

1. Drive in movie theater to see "Mystery Mall"
2. Sandsharks baseball game on 4/28, 29 or 30
3. Go to Green Golf driving range on Elm Street
4. Two mile run around neighborhood
5. Any classical symphony concert - professional or amateur
6. Attend a comedy show at the comedy club on Beltline

● **THINGS I LIKE TO GET**

1. Orange/Vanilla candle from Carter's
2. A case of sparkling water
3. A ream of 28lb printer paper
4. Boxed set of stationary
5. Arranged flowers from florist
6. Salted caramel cupcakes from our neighborhood

Babysitter Info: Shari Clay, 214-555-1212

Overview of the Intentional Date Night Menu

Before we look at each category, there are a few things to note about the Intentional Date Night Menu.

> *There are TWO versions of the Intentional Date Night Menu: a "his" version and a "hers" version.*

- First, there are TWO versions of the Intentional Date Night Menu: a "his" version and a "hers" version. If the wife is planning an Intentional Date Night, she uses her husband's version of the menu and vice versa.

- The Intentional Date Night Menu is a living, breathing document. Notice there is a place at the top of the menu to record the date. Once the menu is initially completed, each spouse makes updates to his or her menu on a regular basis. We recommend updating the menu monthly and holding each other accountable to doing so. Remember: the first time you complete the menu will be the most difficult and the most time-consuming, but updating will be easier.

- Be specific on your date night menu so the host does not need to guess what you want. It's not just a matter of listing "Italian food" in Restaurants I Like to Visit. Instead, write the name of a specific Italian restaurant to leave no room for second-guessing.

- Each category has six blanks to provide options for planning. Fill in each line with specific answers before giving your completed menu to your spouse.

- Each Intentional Date Night will incorporate <u>at least two</u> of the four categories. For instance, you might plan a date that involves your spouse's favorite restaurant plus a place she likes to go. If you use ideas from more than two categories, you have planned a great date!

Restaurants I Like to Visit

Restaurants I Like to Visit is where you list as specifically as possible your six top picks for restaurants. Again, do not list "burger place", instead write "Tom's Burger Shack on Hall Avenue." Take the guesswork out of planning by offering specific options.

A few additional tips:

- *List new or special restaurants.* Try to stay away from the tried and true. Be creative. List the places that would make you feel special. Breaking from the norm will help keep your date night intentional and focused on *getting* your spouse.

- *Choose restaurants that take reservations.* This saves you valuable time, and choosing a restaurant that takes reservations likely isn't one of your go-to places to eat.

- *Keep dress codes in mind.* If you list a restaurant that requires a jacket for men, make a note on the date night menu so your husband has those details when planning a date. Alternatively, if the restaurant encourages throwing peanut shells on the ground, make a note for your wife to leave her best heels at home.

Places I Like to Go

Places I Like to Go are locales — besides restaurants — where you and your spouse aren't confined to a specific time period and can enjoy the place at your own pace. The possibilities are endless, but specificity is key.

Some examples:

- Museums
- Parks
- Historic Sites
- Tourist locations (think stay-cation ideas!)
- Nature trails

Are there opening or closing hours you need to be aware of? Is there an admission fee? Research the place beforehand to make sure all the details are covered. Be sure your Intentional Date Night Menu captures those specifics to help your spouse in planning.

Things I Like to Do

Unlike Places I Like to Go, this category typically involves an organized activity where date and time frame are critical to the planning.

Some examples:

- Sporting events
- Movies
- Theater
- Concerts

Again, you may be tempted to list "baseball game" only. Rather, list the specific team, dates and times.

Lastly, if you choose a specific movie from this category along with a restaurant, attend the movie first before you go to dinner. Doing so takes away the time crunch you might feel of having to make the movie on time and allows for a more relaxed environment for conversation over dinner.

Things I Like to Get

If you really like gifts, then your eyes are lighting up right about now! However, if gifts are not special to you, there is still good reason for our including this as part of the menu.

First, realize there can be joy in both giving and receiving gifts. Receiving gifts may not be important to you, but your spouse can certainly enjoy giving gifts to you.

Secondly, when you purchase a gift for your spouse, it demonstrates you were thinking of him or her when you were apart. You had to take the time, and put forth the energy and effort to purchase the gift in advance. It's not the item that is most important; it's what the item represents.

The parameters for Things I Like to Get are:

- The gift should be something small and within a set budget. We recommend items that are $25 or less for this category. Money will be spent on the date; the gift is a small piece of the overall experience.

- Setting a bar for the gift price forces both you and your spouse to be creative in simple expressions. Again, this is not about surprising your wife with an expensive piece of jewelry. It is about purchasing something from the list she would enjoy and would show you were thinking of her before the date.

Another idea for this part of the menu might be an item you need on a regular basis but you forget to purchase for yourself. For example, Cindy continuously runs out of paper for her printer. Although printer paper is not very romantic, how nice would it be if Tom purchased this for her Things I Like to Get so the next time she runs out, she has some on hand!

Be sure to choose something directly from your spouse's list. The intent is NOT to come up with a new, creative, unexpected gift for your spouse — you can do that on his birthday! The intent is simply to purchase an item to demonstrate your thoughtfulness and love.

Step 3: Ask Your Spouse On Intentional Date Night

Just because you're married doesn't give you the right to lose your manners. Taking time to properly ask your spouse on a date is critical.

You have a lot of latitude when it comes to "the ask." You can be straightforward or creative — whatever best fits your personality.

Key tips for the spouse making "the ask":

- Decide whether your spouse would appreciate knowing the details of the date ahead of time, or if being surprised would be part of the fun.

- Be mindful of dress code. Present any specific needs. For example, if you plan to take a long walk around her favorite lake, be sure she brings a pair of walking shoes.

- Be sure your spouse knows of any rigid time requirements. For example, if you are attending a play, you might want to emphasize what time you need to leave the house in order to arrive at the theater on time for the performance.

Key tips for the spouse receiving "the ask":

- Remember that your spouse has put time and energy into planning this date based on what you like. Share how excited you are about the date and thank your spouse for putting the effort into planning.

- Don't change the day and time of the date. Remember, you agreed to the day and time in Step 1.

- Stick to the original plan, and don't criticize your spouse for choosing certain options over others from your menu. This is your spouse's opportunity to plan a date based on your preferences that she thinks will be pleasing to you.

Step 4: Conversation During Intentional Date Night

Again, *getting* your spouse happens when conversation is intentional and focused on the other person. Intentional Date Nights centered on Restaurants I Like to Eat or Places I Like to Go make great platforms for intentional conversations. However, Intentional Date Nights centered on Things I Like to Do — such as a basketball game or a movie — don't lend themselves as easily to in-depth conversation. Try to have a balance of date activities that allow for conversation to establish connection.

As part of the role as host, the host initiates the conversation. After having invested so much thought and energy into planning the date, we want the same amount of thought and energy invested into connecting with your spouse through conversation.

 Gregg highly recommends to his clients they leave their phones at home. In this day and age that likely sounds impossible, so as hard as it may be, keep those phones in your purse or pocket. Worried that the babysitter may call with an emergency? Simply set your phone on "loud" and then remove it from your line of vision so your focus can be on your spouse. (Refer to our videocast: "Phone at Home" to hear why.)

Remember, the collective purpose on your date is to learn one new thing about your spouse. To do this, the focus of your conversation should be positive and fresh.

Off-limits topics for date-night conversation include:

- Problems or issues in the marriage
- Anxiety or fear
- Children
- Challenges at work

So, if you can't talk about what challenges you have as a couple, what do you talk about? We have three different "conversation catalysts" to spark connection on your date.

Conversation Catalyst #1: "10 Things I Love About You" and Why

This may be the easiest way to begin connecting with your spouse. It's about the two of you sharing aspects you love, admire and appreciate about the other. What makes this conversation rich is you are not only sharing the characteristic you love about your spouse, but *why* you love that characteristic.

For example, you might love your spouse's integrity, but don't stop with one word. Tell your spouse why you love his integrity.

"Tom, one thing I love about you is your integrity. I so admired when you owned your actions at work when the Redding deal fell through. As hard as that was for you, your constant example of integrity is making a huge impact in our family, especially for our children."

Or you might love your spouse's empathy.

"Cindy, one thing I love about you is your empathy for others. I couldn't help but feel so proud of you when you stopped what you were doing to make dinner for Bob and the kids when Tammy broke

her leg. You did exactly what any family would need in that situation. It was really cool to watch you in action."

For some couples, arriving at these ten things will come easier than for others. However, this kind of conversation allows you to hear a compliment or observation from your spouse you may have never heard before.

Conversation Catalyst #2: Conversation Starters

Conversation Starters are a list of thought-provoking questions that allow you to learn something new about your spouse. Some examples include:

- *When you were 16, what did you think you would do professionally as an adult?*

- *What book has had the biggest impact on your life?*

- *If you could have one talent or skill that you do not currently possess, what would it be?*

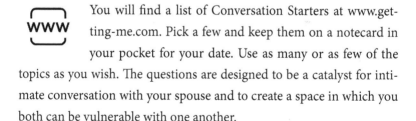 You will find a list of Conversation Starters at www.getting-me.com. Pick a few and keep them on a notecard in your pocket for your date. Use as many or as few of the topics as you wish. The questions are designed to be a catalyst for intimate conversation with your spouse and to create a space in which you both can be vulnerable with one another.

Conversation Catalyst #3: Hopes and Dreams

Often, couples report their best conversations happen during vacation.

Why?

Consider the conditions of a vacation. A couple is out of their normal routine, away from the daily stressors of life, and in an environment that is different from home. These factors subconsciously create an environment that engages our brains to think differently.

On Intentional Date Night, we hope you'll try to create a respite from the routine. Doing so gives you and your spouse the opportunity to discuss all of those thoughts and ideas you want to achieve one day.

Dreaming is not an action plan that must be implemented tomorrow. When we were children, we would dream constantly and share what we wanted to achieve one day. As we mature, we often don't share our dreams so freely because we're fearful of being criticized. At other times, we allow our logic to stunt our dreaming. Think about it: how many times have you started dreaming about an idea and then two minutes into the daydreaming your brain kicks in with "You could never do that!"? As we grow older, we are conditioned not to dream.

Giving your spouse the permission to dream aloud with you is a gift. Allowing them the opportunity to share an idea or a dream with you fully engaged in active listening is powerful. Four questions to jumpstart this conversation include:

- *What would you do if you knew you would not fail?*
- *If time and money were not an object, what is something you would like to do within the next year?*
- *If you had a magic wand and could change any aspect of your life, what would it be and why?*
- *What would you love to see us accomplish by our 25th wedding anniversary?*

Once you ask the question, listen and focus on your spouse's answer in such a way that encourages an intimate conversation to follow. As your spouse shares, continue asking open-ended questions to understand more about the dream. Tell him your observations about the dream and what you like about it. If relevant, discuss if aspects of the dream should ever translate into goals for your spouse or for you both as a couple.

One final note: don't criticize the dream as being unrealistic or not having value. Criticism will shut down intimacy and lead to fear and, often, shame. If your spouse shares something you think is "off the radar," your role is not to criticize but to *get* your spouse.

Step 5: Close Your Intentional Date Night

Once your great date night wraps up, there are a few things to remember as you close your Intentional Date Night:

- If you asked your spouse on the date, be sure you tell him how you enjoyed planning and going on the date.

- If you were invited on the date, be sure you thank her for planning the date.

- Confirm who is planning the next date night — ideally the next date will be within 2-3 weeks.

Sex is not a foregone conclusion with Intentional Date Night. As we discuss in the Pillow Talk conversation, physical intimacy will more likely take place when you both feel connected to one another. If you have been focused on your spouse and engaged in rich conversation, sex may be your shared natural conclusion. However, be respectful if your spouse feels emotionally connected — but not necessarily physically close — following your Intentional Date Night.

Remember the Goal

Remember your goal on Intentional Date Night is to get to know and understand at least one new thing about your spouse — there are bonus points if you learn more than one! Dating your spouse intentionally will help reveal intricacies of you and your spouse that you have not noticed or pursued for years. Don't let familiarity diminish your desire for discovery or get in the way of spending quality time with each other. If your once beloved date nights have been hijacked by a mere way to skip the kids' bedtime routine, it's time for a change.

We hope this approach will not only allow for great dates with your spouse, but will refresh a sense of excitement that grows you closer, regardless of how many years you have been together. And we believe this purposeful approach to dating is a proven way to *get* your spouse in fun and creative ways.

NEXT STEPS

- Each person needs to complete the Intentional Date Night Menu. You can find an Intentional Date Night Menu template at www.getting-me.com.

- Discuss who will host the first date.

- If you are hosting the date, remember to plan a date using your spouse's Intentional Date Night Menu preferences.

- Ask your spouse on the date.

- Think about how you want to spark conversation that will drive connection on the date.

- Talk about a plan for how you will keep your Intentional Date Night menu current and refreshed at least every 30 days. Make a commitment to one another to try Intentional Date Night for at least three months to give yourselves the opportunity to build this marital habit.

REFLECTION QUESTIONS

1. What is the latest "discovery" I have made about my spouse? In other words, when was the last time we were able to connect in such a way that we learned a new hope, dream or characteristic of one another that we had not known previously?

2. What will make it difficult for us as a couple to actually go on an Intentional Date Night? What can we do to proactively address those obstacles?

3. What do we find interesting about the Intentional Date Night approach? How can we use that interest as motivation to maintain this marital habit between us as a couple?

4. After attending an Intentional Date Night, reflect on what you liked about the night. What pleasant surprises did you encounter? What did you discover new about each other?

Comings and Goings

A typical day in the life of Amy and George:

6:00 a.m.   *George wakes up and goes to the gym. Amy answers email and reviews social media.*

7:00 a.m.   *Both get dressed for work in their master bathroom facing their own sink and mirror. Amy confirms that George will be ready for a 7:00 p.m. dinner with her work colleagues. Their conversation centers on what each has on their work agenda for the day. George is the first to leave; he wishes Amy a good day and walks out the front door by 7:45 a.m. Amy leaves for work at 8:00 a.m.*

11:30 a.m.   *George texts Amy to ask if she can pick up the family dog at the veterinarian after work; she replies "yes."*

2:00 p.m.   *Amy sends George an email with the name of the restaurant for dinner along with which of her colleagues will attend; George does not reply.*

6:00 p.m. *Amy arrives at home after picking up the dog; George is not home. She begins to dress for dinner, continuously watching the clock. At 6:25, Amy texts George.*

Amy: "Where are you?"

George: "At work."

Amy: "What?! I told you dinner was at 7."

George: "No, you said I needed to be ready by 7. I thought that's when I needed to be dressed and ready to go."

Amy: "I can't believe this. Just meet me there. Details are in your inbox."

10:30 p.m. *Amy and George arrive home in separate cars after dinner. As they prepare for bed, their conversation turns to what they each thought of the evening out. No mention was made of the miscommunication they experienced before dinner. They get into bed and, after watching 30 minutes of television, turn off the TV, say "goodnight" and roll over.*

When Conversations Don't Create Connection

A vast majority of the conversations spouses have each day are something like Amy and George's. If you had a transcript of all the conversations you had with your spouse yesterday, chances are you'd find most took place before leaving for work and when you returned home. Perhaps a few conversations were had during the work day — by phone, email or text — but those were probably brief. The content of your conversations likely centered around sharing stories from the day, logistics of the week and small talk. These types of conversations are the kind that neither you nor your spouse count as meaningful conversation. Most marital conversations occur when a couple is "coming" or "going."

This kind of brief communication dynamic only increases for couples with kids. Morning conversations diminish even more so with every additional person added to the household. If it wasn't hard enough with just the two of you, now you have little Sammy who just spilled his bowl of cereal, while your teenager is leaving for school wearing the t-shirt you asked him to throw away. The chances for conversation have been reduced to almost zero.

> *The days are so full with responsibility that most couples don't take the time to connect intentionally on a regular basis.*

The days are so full with responsibility that most couples don't take the time to connect intentionally on a regular basis. Most conversations during the day are made up of logistics regarding schedules, meals or household errands. The end of the day is usually a flurry of preparing dinner, doing homework and trying to ensure the kids are in bed by a reasonable time.

While couples may talk to one another multiple times a day, very rarely do these conversations create a sense of connection. This can produce forced timing for a spouse if he has something that must be discussed. Desperate for a moment of connection, couples often find re-entry and departure times (or Comings and Goings) become breeding grounds for arguments because someone is trying to address topics that don't fit in the constraints of the time and space. For instance, vocalizing your hurt feelings from a recent comment made by an in-law cannot be resolved in the time it takes to get ready for work!

For marriages striving for a meaningful, daily connection, we suggest that Comings and Goings are moments that need to be reexamined and approached in a completely different way.

What are Comings and Goings?

Comings and Goings refer to the conversations spouses have at different points in the day: when they *depart* from one another, when they are *apart* from one another and when they *reunite* with one another. These conversations have a direct effect on our sense of security. Because the more we *get* one another — and show we love, appreciate and respect one another — the more secure we feel as a result. How you connect when you leave one another or when you reunite can give a sense of how the marriage is doing.

The way we interact with one another as we come and go is an opportunity to show how we *get* one another. When you leave in the morning by kissing your spouse and saying "I hope you have a great day," you depart feeling more secure than the days you leave your spouse after a heated argument. Even in the casual moments of passing one another in your home, when you don't acknowledge the other in some way — either by word or touch — you miss an opportunity to create a connection. At re-entry after a work day, when spouses do not acknowledge each other, one or both of you run the risk of feeling undervalued, unloved and unappreciated.

> *Comings and Goings refer to the conversations spouses have at different points in the day: when they **depart** from one another, when they are **apart** from one another and when they **reunite** with one another.*

Comings and Goings moments present the greatest opportunities for connection in a marriage. By learning the best way to interact with one another in these moments, you naturally grow in *getting* one another. The more you start to *get* one another, the more you foster a sense of stability and security in the marriage. Couples must be more intentional when coming and going. Learning how to interact when you *depart*, are *apart*, and when you *reunite* will help you both feel heard, understood and known.

How can you "come and go" better as a couple?

Four Times of Comings and Goings

Every couple, regardless of how long they've been married or if they have children, experience four times throughout each day when they can intentionally connect. These opportunities focus on the spouse who is either the "first" or the "last" in the activity, and the intentional steps to seek out the other to connect. If approached deliberately, these situations can foster a sense of connection. The four times of Comings and Goings are:

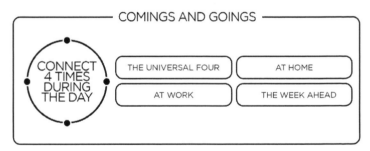

Coming and Going #1: The Universal Four

The Universal Four are moments you're already experiencing as a couple. To improve these moments, we suggest you approach each one with a greater purpose. Here's how:

Much like childhood bedtime routines that create security, we are suggesting routines for waking up, bedtime, leaving home, and coming home that plant seeds of connection for the day.

The first moment is **waking up.** The <u>last</u> person who wakes up is responsible for finding his spouse to greet with a kind word (for example, "Good morning, how did you sleep?") and a physical touch — a hug, shoulder rub or kiss. This creates a brief moment for the couple to connect in a meaningful way.

As the morning unfolds, many couples spend the first hour getting ready for daily activities in a shared bathroom. Even these seemingly insignificant moments are tone-setters for the day. Be respectful of the fact that the "getting ready" time is not the place to launch into complex or challenging conversations that deserve time and space for intentional discussion. Conversation during this getting-ready time should be light and free of discussing marital issues or attempting to resolve conflict.

Leaving home at the beginning of the day follows a similar pattern. The <u>first</u> person leaving needs to seek out the other and wish him/her a good day. Why is this so important? Consider this scenario:

Mark was running late for work, while Elizabeth was feeding their two kids breakfast. One child seemed especially grumpy, and Elizabeth quickly realized his forehead was hot and his face looked pale. She took the child's temperature and was studying the thermometer when Mark dashed around the kitchen corner almost in a run. He shouted

"Bye!" to everyone and slammed the back door. Elizabeth stared at the closed door amazed. Mark didn't realize one of their children was not feeling well, nor did he acknowledge a single member of his family as he left.

Too many couples begin their day without ever connecting. This sets the tone of the day for both of you. Much like a football player who is sent from the sidelines into the game, his teammates don't ignore him as he does; they encourage him and cheer him on as he takes the field. Likewise, a connected couple should see their collective role as sending one another onto the "field" of life, whether it's leaving the security of their home for the day or staying to manage the family.

We believe it is extremely important to leave your home with great intention <u>each</u> day. The first one to leave needs to seek out the other to ensure a kind word and moment is shared as the last moment of being together before reuniting.

> *We believe it is extremely important to leave your home with great intention <u>each</u> day.*

Coming home at the end of the day is another important connection point. The <u>last</u> person arriving home must find his or her spouse to make an intentional connection — before connecting with the kids, the dog or reading the mail. Once you have made a connection, with a kind word and a non-sexual touch, then you can allow time to separate to decompress.

One important tip for working spouses: pick a physical marker in your commute home — a restaurant, a certain street or a billboard — that serves as a signal to mentally leave work behind and transition your focus to your husband or wife. Each time you pass it, discipline yourself

CONVERSATION 2 — COMINGS AND GOINGS

to change your focus to your home life. This simple tip can change your mindset long before you open the front door at the end of a demanding day.

One important tip for stay-at-home spouses or spouses who work from home: pick an action to take 15 minutes before your spouse comes home that signals it's time to mentally shift to your spouse. When your spouse arrives home, stop what you're doing — whether with your kids or work — to take the time to intentionally connect with him or her. Stay at home parents, resist the urge to hand off the kid-baton as soon as your spouse walks in the door.

At **Bedtime**, it is the <u>first</u> person going to bed that needs to seek out their spouse to end the day in the same manner the day began: verbally and in a physical, non-sexual way. The day should end with goodnight pleasantries, coupled with a kiss or a hug.

Coming and Going #2: At Home

It may seem strange to consider a Coming and Going when both of you are in the home. But we've discovered doing so presents two opportunities: one to intentionally connect and one to intentionally avoid conflict.

Passing in the Home

Let's say you and your spouse are home but in different rooms. How many times might you cross each other without even acknowledging the other's presence? Too often, you might walk through the kitchen while your spouse is doing dishes or walk through the living room while your spouse is reading and not even acknowledge him or her. These times offer a simple, brief moment to connect intentionally as you come and go.

Consider this scenario:

Steve walks past Ann in the kitchen as she is doing the dishes. He pauses and looks at her for a few seconds as he is sure he had something to tell her, but, for the life of him, can't remember what it is. He shrugs his shoulders and moves on to the living room.

Whether you realize it or not, your spouse attaches a meaning to every nonverbal you share. Just imagine the meaning Ann could attach to Steve's nonverbals! *Steve pauses, looks at Ann, makes no comments, and then shrugs his shoulders.* So many thoughts could easily cross Ann's mind: "he doesn't care about me," "he doesn't even appreciate that I'm doing the dishes," "he is too selfish to help," etc. But from Steve's point of view, this was an innocent chain of events that occurs in a person's mind — basic forgetfulness! Regardless, Ann could misinterpret his nonverbals all too easily. This misinterpretation is, at best, a missed opportunity to connect, and, at worst, an opportunity for conflict.

> *Whether you realize it or not, your spouse attaches a meaning to every nonverbal you share.*

Now, read the same scenario with a different twist:

Steve walks past Ann in the kitchen as she is doing the dishes. He pauses and looks at her for a few seconds as he is sure he had something to tell her, but, for the life of him, can't remember what it is. As Ann catches his glance, Steve switches gears and says, "Hey, I had something I wanted to tell you but I can't remember what it was! So, while my old brain kicks into gear, can I help you with those dishes?"

How completely different is Ann's reaction! Steve took what seems like an unimportant moment in the home and used it to connect. Although his original purpose was to walk into the kitchen and tell Ann something that was important to him, he transforms the purpose into a time to offer help, which immediately makes a connection.

Please don't misunderstand what we are suggesting. By no means are we saying that each time you see your spouse at home you must connect. We do recommend, however, that as often as you can, you seek to use the ordinary, everyday moments to create moments of connection. You will be completely surprised at what a wink, a touch, a "can I help?" or "how's it going?" can do to make for a great moment of connection with your spouse.

Engaged State in the Home

Perhaps the greatest breeding ground for arguments is when both spouses are home but one of you is in what we call an "engaged state" — meaning intently focused on something that does not involve the other. For instance, watching an important football game, studying for a professional exam or working on a hobby. Too often, the "unengaged" spouse does not recognize that these are not the times to start a deep conversation, but are the times to demonstrate respect and allow your engaged spouse to have his/her individual time. Let Chris and Nancy's scenario explain further:

Nancy hangs up the phone with the seventh-grade teacher after a 30-minute conversation about her son's failing grades. Full of worry, Nancy seeks out Chris to discuss. She finds him in the living room fully engaged in watching a football game. "Chris," Nancy says as she stands in front of the TV, "we have to talk about David's grades. His teacher just called and he is failing seventh grade!"

Chris's response? "Ok, let me get to halftime and then we'll discuss. I can't miss this game."

Outraged, Nancy replies, "You're telling me that football is more important than your son? No wonder he is failing out of school, considering how little you care about his well-being!"

So what has happened?

- Nancy is worried and anxious after receiving bad news from a teacher. She immediately wants to share this anxiety with her husband for her own relief.

- Nancy seeks out Chris, thinking he's just watching a football game, never realizing he is in the middle of something important to him.

- When Nancy begins to speak, Chris responds with "I can . . . but not right now."

- Nancy becomes infuriated and then makes unfair conclusions about Chris because he won't begin a conversation with her right then and there.

On the surface, Nancy is furious that Chris won't start the conversation immediately. But, at the core, Nancy fears that Chris doesn't *get* her and how important this is to her. While her response is valid, there are two important things spouses need to remember when they are both at home:

- There will be times when each person is in an *engaged state* at home. Whether watching television or involved in a hobby, each spouse needs specific, uninterrupted time that the other spouse honors and respects.

- Each couple needs to discuss how to approach the other when in an *engaged state*.

How can you respond when you need to talk to your spouse but he is in an *engaged state*? First, recognize that he is focused on something important to him. Politely interrupt, simply state your need, and then ask when would be a good time to discuss the issue. Consider this better approach when Nancy needed to talk to Chris:

"Chris, I know you are in the middle of watching the game and I don't want to interrupt. I just got a phone call from David's teacher, and I need to discuss it with you. When would be a good time to do that?"

You might be surprised by how this approach could open an immediate conversation. And even if it doesn't, this approach shows your respect for your spouse and creates a time for when he will be ready to engage in conversation with you. By respecting and understanding the significance of your spouse's engaged state — you show that you *get* your spouse.

Coming and Going #3: At Work

Since working couples often spend more than 40 hours a week apart, it is very important for a couple to discuss when, how and how often they will connect during the work day. Too often, Gregg has seen a "lack of communication about communication" create conflict for couples. One spouse may believe he has full access to his wife at work, while the wife doesn't want to be interrupted. Couples need to discuss the guidelines of communicating during the work day.

Here are a few questions to consider as a couple:

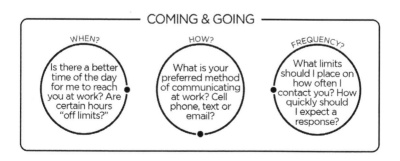

COMING & GOING

WHEN? Is there a better time of the day for me to reach you at work? Are certain hours "off limits?"

HOW? What is your preferred method of communicating at work? Cell phone, text or email?

FREQUENCY? What limits should I place on how often I contact you? How quickly should I expect a response?

These questions are simple, but they serve as a healthy and strong framework for a couple to determine how they are going to handle communications when apart from one another.

A word of caution about email and text between you and your spouse: because of their ease and efficiency, email and text can easily become a primary method of communication during the work day. But too often, email and text become a shield to hide behind when a tough voice-to-voice or face-to-face conversation needs to be had. It is too easy to fire off an

> *Our recommendation is that email and text is used ONLY for logistics and positive comments.*

angry email to your spouse at work when neither of you have the opportunity to unpack and resolve the issue.

Our recommendation is that email and text is used ONLY for logistics and positive comments. Use these to communicate a meeting place or time, or to say something complimentary to your spouse. Using email or text to share a concern or make an angry statement is only placing a match to a can of gasoline!

www Lastly, for the couple who has a spouse that travels frequently, this "At Work" Coming and Going moment must be discussed in depth. Some couples use Skype or FaceTime as a temporary way to connect. To connect in a more tangible way, you may consider writing a note and secretly slipping it in your spouse's suitcase. Surprising your spouse with a special dessert delivered to her hotel room is yet another way to relate across the miles. Business travel is the enemy of marital connection. Discuss how you will intentionally connect *each day* if one of you is traveling for business. (Refer to our videocast: "Business Travel and Marriage" for more.)

Coming and Going #4: The Week Ahead

Perhaps the greatest assurance for better Comings and Goings for a couple is The Week Ahead meeting. The Week Ahead meeting allows a couple to look at the next six days to ensure each person not only knows the schedule ahead, but to proactively work out any potential scheduling conflicts. Having a shared knowledge of the logistics of the week ahead makes the "going" time of getting ready in the morning simply an affirmation of what was previously discussed.

Whether taking place on Saturdays or Sundays, this meeting allows the couple — in a scheduled, intentional time — to discuss expectations for the week, whether it be joint engagements or individual responsibilities. When a couple is connected logistically, it can help them feel connected emotionally. For example, if the wife knows her husband has an important work meeting that week, it offers her the opportunity to support, encourage and pray for him specifically in the week.

The Week Ahead meeting is a schedule and logistics conversation. Here is an example of what The Week Ahead discussion could look like:

COMINGS AND GOINGS

SCHEDULE: Any special events you need the other to know about? Any late night work nights? Early morning meetings? Events you both need to attend?

- *Kylie's ballet recital on Thursday at 6:00 p.m.*
- *Kim: Working out on Wednesday at 5:30 a.m.*
- *Bob: Working late on Tuesday, home after 8:00 p.m.*

LOGISTICS: Special tasks or errand that need to be handled this week?

- *Pick up dry cleaning on Wednesday (Bob)*
- *Drop meal off at Sandy's on Thursday (Kim)*

LONG-TERM VIEW: Any special events, projects or tasks that are upcoming in the month that you need the other to know about?

- *Company gala on March 22 at 8:00 p.m.; attire is black tie*
- *Kitchen renovation demo starts on March 30 -- room needs to be emptied*

Each couple will devise their own topics for the weekly meeting. These 30 minutes or less of touching base before the week begins will ward off a great deal of frustration and confusion for the six days to follow.

Helpful Tips for Comings and Goings

There are a few things to consider each time you and your spouse depart from and reunite with one another, regardless of when the Comings and Goings occur:

- When you depart/reunite, ensure you look at each other in the eye, be in close proximity to one another and touch each other in a non-sexual way.

- Even though the Comings and Goings time may be brief, pay attention to one another and be attentive in your listening.

- When you reconnect, instead of asking "How was your day?" ask "How are you doing?" Resist using "fine" as an answer. Instead, try to answer in three complete sentences. The listening spouse then picks one of the sentences he or she heard and uses that as a springboard for further conversation. For example:

Mary: "How are you doing?"

Scott: "I am tired. I am frustrated by work. And I really need a vacation."

Mary: "Tell me more about why you are frustrated by work. What's going on there?"

With Scott replying in three complete sentences, Mary can dive into a deeper conversation about something that is important and relevant to him. This simple technique can take your communication to a deeper level fairly quickly if the listener is attentive and curious.

Remember the Goal

Remember the goal of Comings and Goings is to interact daily with your spouse in intentional ways that show you *get* one another. Many everyday conversations you have during the day may seem unimportant and inconsequential. However, it's in these brief moments of connecting that create opportunities to hear, understand and know one another. When a couple intentionally connects throughout the day they are building an even greater, more meaningful connection within their marriage. The more you *get* one another, the more secure your marriage will feel.

NEXT STEPS

- Be intentional about The Universal Four. Pick one of the moments — waking up, bedtime, leaving home or coming home — and for the next week focus on connecting in that moment.

- Discuss what you do well as a couple when At Home and what could be improved. Are you good at giving each other personal space or time when needed? How will you communicate to one another when you are in an *engaged state*?

- Commit to one another that you will hold The Week Ahead meeting for four weeks in a row. Be intentional about observing if this planning meeting decreases miscommunications in your week.

REFLECTION QUESTIONS

1. How would we rate how we depart and reunite daily as a couple? Which Coming and Going moment is strong in our approach? Which Coming and Going moment do we want to improve?

2. What makes each of us feel most secure when we leave our home and take the "field" of life and daily responsibilities?

3. What are our guidelines for communicating with one another while at work?

4. When do we want to have our first The Week Ahead meeting? What day/time would be best for us to have that meeting?

Couch Time

"It's been a terrible week," Beth moaned to her friend, Lisa, over Saturday morning coffee. "A terrible week."

"Why?" Lisa asked.

"This entire week seemed like one long, heated argument with Frank. Monday began with him asking me — while I was getting ready for work, mind you — why we had run out of cereal. I told him, 'Last time I checked, he could drive too . . . why was getting groceries only my responsibility?' He looked at me blankly, left the bathroom, and didn't speak to me for the rest of the morning."

"Wow," Lisa responded.

Beth continued, "Then on Wednesday, I paid the bills and again, we have charged more on our Visa than we had agreed to — specifically, Frank spent over $1,000 on golf gear! How can you spend $1,000 on golf gear? When I asked him about it, he quickly reminded me that he earns more money than me, and he should be able to bust the budget every now and then. I told him this is the fourth time he has busted the budget this year — and it's only May! He then blew up on me, saying that I was micro-managing him again, and all he wants is this one aspect of his life left to himself. I told him maybe living at the golf club with those girls that drive the carts would be better than living with me. And he quickly replied, 'Don't think I haven't thought of that.'"

"You've got to be kidding me," Lisa exclaimed. "You've talked to Frank about his spending more than once. Why can't he understand that he needs to stick to what you agreed to for his so-called hobby?"

Beth nodded, grateful for the validation. But, she wasn't done.

"And then last night — get this! I'm in the kitchen, cleaning dishes that literally had been in the sink since Wednesday. We had tickets for a seven o'clock movie. I thought a mindless comedy was exactly what we needed after having been at each other's throats all week. It was an hour before we had to leave; we had plenty of time for me to finish cleaning the kitchen and get to the theater. Frank came in, saw me, and lost it . . . again."

Beth relayed the conversation for Lisa with great clarity:

> Frank: "Are you ready to go?"
>
> Beth: "I need to finish these dishes and then we can go."
>
> Frank: "Why are you trying to sabotage this evening?"
>
> Beth: "Sabotage? What do you mean?"
>
> Frank: (With a glare in his eye, he started shouting) "We've been married 10 years and you know that I hate walking into a movie late. I'm not sure how you don't get this simple fact about me. It's not hard to remember. I LIKE TO BE AT THE MOVIES EARLY!"

Lisa laughed at Beth's reenactment of the story. "Unbelievable! So, what did you do?"

"I just stopped washing the dishes, grabbed my purse and went and sat in the car — all without saying a word. Then, in his brilliant passive-aggressive way, he took his time in the house and made me wait in the car for five minutes before he came out. We drove to the movie in silence. And although the movie was really funny, I barely laughed because I was so angry."

Beth sighed heavily. "But as the movie progressed, my feelings turned from anger to fear. I reflected on the week and started wondering, 'Is our marriage falling apart? It seems like we argue more than we don't.'"

Lisa didn't know how to respond, but she couldn't help but think the same.

Does this scene sound familiar? When you dissect Beth and Frank's arguments, their issues are fairly common: responsibility, money and time. What is also fairly common is *how* they argued about their issues: on-the-spot, fueled by emotion, and with a deep desire to prove their own self as "right" and the other as "wrong." In the case of Beth and Frank, their arguing had become a pattern of their regular behavior, instead of being the exception to the rule.

What role does arguing play in your marriage? If you share a similar argument pattern as Beth and Frank — how can you break this harmful pattern?

Why Couples Fight

Married couples tend to argue with two primary objectives: to prove "I am right and you are wrong," and to force their spouse to agree with their point of view.

The pursuit of victory seems to be foundational to every marital argument. Consider the last three arguments you've had with your spouse. Regardless of the issue, did you find yourself seeking peace or seeking to prove you were right? Would you be willing to admit that you couldn't even consider the argument over until your spouse agreed with you? This can be a never-ending battle if you both share this same self-serving objective.

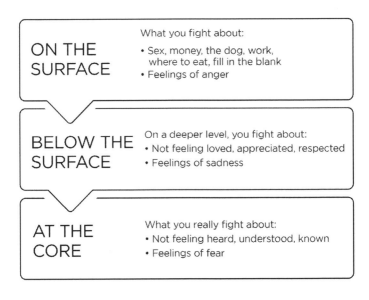

As you may remember from chapter two, what we fight about is not what we are *really* fighting about. When couples fight, the underlying factor of the argument is not *really* about cereal, or golf gear, or missing the previews, but is a fear of not feeling heard, understood, known. Your core fear being that your spouse does not *get* you.

For instance, when Frank's reaction was over the top about being late to the movie (yelling, "*I LIKE TO BE AT THE MOVIES EARLY!*"), you may have judged his behavior as extreme. Or maybe you, too, have been the over-reactor. On the surface, Frank seemed crazy to argue so strongly about missing the previews. Yet when you consider the arguments

> *What we fight about is not what we are **really** fighting about.*

they had throughout the week, Frank's outrageous reaction had been building since Monday.

Recall Frank's week from his perspective:

- On Monday morning, he wanted cereal and there was none in the pantry. He interpreted this lack of food as Beth not wanting to take care of his needs. Therefore, he did not feel loved by Beth.

- On Wednesday afternoon, Beth criticized him for his golf spending. He immediately felt unappreciated as the primary provider in their home.

- On Friday night, when Beth was cleaning the kitchen when he was ready to go, Frank exploded. He needed Beth to respect his need to be early to the movies. And after 10 years, he was appalled she still didn't *get* him.

Was Frank right to explode? He was fed up. Wasn't his reaction justified, since he had sensed all week Beth's lack of love and respect for him? However, if Frank had been able to consider alternative logic — that the missing cereal was a simple oversight, or that Beth's observation about his over-spending was strictly a financial issue, not a personal one — he may not have exploded. Instead, Frank's impulsive reaction created a poor environment for their hearing, understanding, and knowing one another. When conflict arises, *getting* one another is critical to finding a helpful resolution.

Let's reflect on *how* arguments typically happen:

- Arguments begin with strong feelings (typically anger) versus logic.

- Arguments are driven by the person who needs to release that anger with no consideration of the spouse's readiness to deal with the circumstances at hand.

Every marriage will have its share of arguments. That's normal. However, most arguments are not constructive, and appear to be more of a dueling match between two people who only want to prove how right they are! It doesn't have to be this way. We believe there is a way to completely transform *how* you argue. You may want to sit down for this.

What if you viewed every argument as a wonderful platform to <u>create</u> <u>intimacy</u>? You may be asking yourself, when have the words *wonderful* or *intimacy* ever been used to describe arguing? But, what if you approached a conflict with the goal of *getting* one another instead of winning one another over? Imagine if every issue over which you and your spouse argue, drew you closer to one another — not further apart.

WWW Imagine if in that millisecond when your brain fires off "Let's fight!", you chose instead to say "Let's have Couch Time." Meaning, what if in that millisecond, instead of reacting impulsively, you suspended your emotional response in order to resolve conflict through an intentional conversation? This would completely transform the way you two argue. (Refer to our videocast: "Why Suspending Emotion is Easier Said than Done" for more.)

What is Couch Time?

Couch Time is a scheduled conversation couples use to resolve conflict in their marriage. This arranged time set apart to discuss problems, replaces unproductive, hot-tempered, on-the-spot arguments.

As the name suggests, this conversation occurs on a couch or in a place where both spouses can face each other, look into each other's eyes, and are in close enough proximity to touch. Couch Time has a brief agenda with one or two items to discuss. Each item will be a challenging topic that is a source of conflict in the marriage and creates feelings of anger, sadness or fear for one or both spouses in the marriage. Couch Time should be no longer than 45 minutes, as the conversation will be intense.

> *Couch Time is a scheduled conversation couples use to resolve conflict in their marriage.*

Couch Time gives you the place and space to deal with conflict in a new way, and with a new goal: to *get* your spouse. The goal is not to prove you are right and your spouse is wrong.

By approaching the Couch Time conversation with the goal of *getting* one another, you listen in such a way that you can get inside your spouse's mind and see the circumstances from his or her point of view rather than your own.

This is a revolutionary concept because it is completely counter-cultural. In Western culture, arguing is about winning. In Eastern culture, it is about blending two views to create a stronger outcome — think *yin and yang*. With this in mind, when conflict arises, don't engage with the emotion right then and there. Rather, pause, schedule a time to address the circumstances, and then calmly engage in Couch Time.

Couch Time will not only help you resolve conflict in a constructive way, but will develop deeper intimacy with your spouse.

The Key to Couch Time

Getting your spouse is the ability to see the world through his or her eyes. Therefore, when conflict arises, the key to Couch Time is seeking to understand your spouse first, instead of forcing your own understanding.

Think about it: what would happen if the next time you experience conflict with your spouse you suspended your own desire to win and sought to first understand why your spouse was so angry? How might that conflict be resolved more quickly and more effectively?

You may be thinking, "There is absolutely no way I can't be angry when my spouse ignores me while he's watching TV!" It's natural to be angry. But could you handle your anger in a different way? Whether you recognize it or not, you already know how to do this.

For those in a professional setting, when your boss makes you angry you don't say what you *really* want to say; you use techniques to communicate your differences. When someone you respect outside your home offends you, you communicate thoughtfully to ensure your emotions don't erupt. You can extend that same courtesy to your spouse.

The healthiest marriages are the ones that have the ability to suspend anger in order to engage in understanding. In Couch Time, we want you and your spouse to create a space and place for you to hear each other. Again, the objective of Couch Time is not to win the argument. The objective of Couch Time is to be committed to understanding how the issue impacts your spouse so that it readily leads you to a place of working together for resolution.

> *When conflict arises, the key to Couch Time is seeking to understand your spouse first, instead of forcing your own understanding.*

With this in mind, here's how to have a Couch Time conversation.

How to Have Couch Time

In Gregg's office, Couch Time is the conflict resolution method he asks married couples to adopt to work through issues. This method takes self-control, patience, time, practice, energy, effort, repetition, commitment, discipline, empathy, and compassion. Yes, all of them! You have likely not used all these qualities at once before. And though not easy, Couch Time is a revolutionary and healthy way of resolving conflict in marriage, and well worth the effort.

> *The healthiest marriages are the ones that have the ability to suspend anger in order to engage in understanding.*

For the sake of illustrating the Couch Time process, we are going to use an example of conflict in the marriage of Paul and Natalie:

Paul and Natalie have owned their dog, Max, for three years. Paul loves Max, but Natalie wants to get rid of him. Max has behavioral issues that have been identified, but no action has been taken. Paul has an emotional attachment to Max and is not bothered by the dog's behavior. And although Paul takes care of the dog when he can, he travels for work often, leaving the untrained dog with Natalie. Max's behavior is a major stressor for Natalie. She feels inconvenienced when she has to stop her own activities to take care of Max. She is also bothered by the fact that Max is largely responsible for their house being messy.

Last Wednesday, Natalie walked into the dining room, and felt something squish under her toes. Much to her dismay, she found Max had soiled her most valuable Persian rug. She became instantly furious, not only at the dog, but at Paul. However, she didn't storm off to tell Paul about what she had just literally walked into, but cleaned up the mess in frustrated tears, resolving to schedule a Couch Time with Paul.

Natalie chose not to scream at Paul in the moment. She used patience and self-control, as she decided she wanted to save the conversation for Couch Time. Instead of engaging in a heated argument, she decided to use the conflict as an opportunity for deeper intimacy with Paul. Natalie displayed great discipline when confronted with one of the most difficult challenges of Couch Time: making the choice to have one, instead of acting impulsively.

Here are three steps for a productive Couch Time conversation:

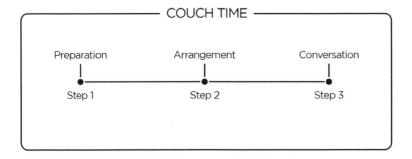

Step 1:   Preparation

The first step is to prepare for a Couch Time conversation. When anxiety or anger hits in a marriage, we all tend to want to talk about it right then and there. It is this sense of urgency and emotion that is often the fuel of an argument. Preparation is necessary.

Before you ask your spouse for a Couch Time meeting, consider the following:

- **Ensure you are calm about the issue.** Allow yourself time to "self-soothe" before the conversation. Do not go into it emotionally-charged.

- **Determine what the end will look like.** Remember the goal is for you to communicate in such a way that your spouse *gets* you and to reach some level of compromise.

- How will you explain the issue in such a way that your spouse can see it from your point of view?

- What questions will you ask of your spouse to help you understand his or her point of view?

- **Be aware of the tone and nonverbals you will use during the conversation.** Remember that good communication takes into account more than your words.

- **Create an opening statement and practice saying it.** The opening statement sets the tone for the entire conversation. It should state the issues clearly, be non-threatening, and begin with how you are feeling.

  In this instance, Natalie's opening statement could sound like this:

  "Paul, I have a problem with the dog. I need you to hear how Max affects me. It's important to me that you know that I love you and I want us to work together to find a solution. Can I share what I'm thinking?"

Once you have prepared for the conversation, you are ready to ask your spouse for Couch Time.

Step 2: Arrangement

The second step is to arrange the details for a Couch Time conversation. The time and location for the conversation is critical to the success.

- **Set Couch Time for a specific time and location.** The location should be a private place, in which you and your spouse can look at each other eye to eye, and sit in close enough proximity to have the ability to touch one another. Gregg has found that when a couple sits on the loveseat in his office, they use the close proximity for a soft touch on the arm to show care and affection for one another.

- **The location should be free of distractions such as kids, television, technology and phones.** Your focus should be exclusively on your spouse and what it is he or she is sharing.

- **Couch Time should last no longer than 45 minutes.** By giving the conversation an end time you reduce the risk of getting overwhelmed and exhausted by the content. If you are worried that the conversation might run over 45 minutes, set a timer! If your Couch Time is not resolved in 45 minutes, set another Couch Time to pick up where you left off.

- **Resist scheduling Couch Time when either one or both of you are tired, hungry or stressed.** Gregg recommends not scheduling a Couch Time for after 8:00 p.m. You want to both be refreshed and ready when you start the conversation.

Here's how Natalie asks Paul for Couch Time:

After dinner, Natalie looked at Paul and said, "I would really like to set a Couch Time with you to discuss the dog. I'd like to have the conversation before the end of the weekend. I'm wondering if we might have coffee on the back porch on Saturday morning around 9:00 a.m.? I think we can have this conversation in less than an hour. Would that work for you?"

Paul, a little stunned by the request, replied, "I guess so, but I want to sleep in. Can it be later?"

Natalie calmly replied, "Sure, how about 11 then?" Paul agreed.

With the arrangements set, you are ready to have a Couch Time conversation.

Step 3:   Conversation

We will refer to the one who initiated the Couch Time as the Speaker. At the start of Couch Time, the Speaker needs to keep the following in mind:

- Thank your spouse for taking the time to hear you. Acknowledge something positive about your marriage and positive characteristics of your spouse.

- **WWW** Open in prayer, and ask God to help you both have ears to hear Him and each other in the conversation. (Refer to our videocast: "Inviting God to Couch Time" to hear more.)

- Remind your spouse that you love him or her and that your objective is not to win the argument, but rather to share how you feel about the topic at hand.

- Be vulnerable. Acknowledge your feelings. If you are nervous, say so.

- Begin the conversation with your opening statement.

- Explain what you hope the outcome of Couch Time will be. For example, "I just want you to understand me" or "I hope we will be able to come to a resolution."

We will refer to the one who was invited to the Couch Time as the Listener. At the start of Couch Time, the Listener needs to keep the following in mind:

- Be open minded and empathetic. Assume the position of trying to understand your spouse rather than getting your point across. Suspend judgment.

- Do not interrupt. Respond when your spouse gives you the opportunity.

- Show genuine interest. Your goal is to show your spouse that you *get* him or her. Listen with a posture of care and love. Remind yourself as you listen that your spouse is the person you love.

- Once the Speaker finishes, the Listener's role is to:

  - Acknowledge you understand how important it is that your spouse feels heard and understood.

  - Restate the feelings you heard — mad, sad, glad or fear?

  - Restate the issue you heard.

  - Ask questions if you need clarification.

  - Ask if your spouse felt heard and understood. At this point you are not agreeing or resolving the issue, you are simply demonstrating that you understand how the issue impacts your spouse.

Allow Natalie and Paul to demonstrate what Couch Time can look like:

Saturday morning finally arrived. Seated in their wooden rockers facing each other, with coffee in hand, Natalie started Couch Time with Paul.

"You may notice my coffee cup slipping out of my hands," Natalie laughed nervously. "It's because my palms are sweating."

Paul leaned back in his chair, "I'm nervous, too."

Natalie started. "Paul, thank you for taking the time to discuss the dog. I so appreciate your willingness to look at this issue again, despite the fact that I get so emotional on this topic so quickly. It's important to me that you know that I love you and I want us to work together to find a solution. As you know, I have a problem with Max. I need you to hear how he affects me. Can I share with you what I'm thinking?"

"Sure," Paul replied, then added, "but I can't imagine what Max has done to bring us to this."

Natalie resisted the urge to snap back, but mustered the self-control to continue. "On Wednesday, I was barefoot walking through the dining room and I walked straight into Max's mess. Right in it, all between my toes. After I cleaned my feet, I went to clean the rug, which you remember is my family's heirloom Persian rug.

"So, here is my problem. Yet again, Max has caused issues for me. He continues to use the bathroom in random places in the house. He has stained the carpet in our bedroom, and now the Persian rug. It took me 30 minutes to wash my feet and the rug — both of which will never be the same. I was in the middle of preparing for my Thursday morning meeting, and I lost 30 minutes of prep time because of a dog. I am just so over Max. He is ruining our house because he is not potty-trained, not to mention that he barks incessantly when he doesn't have you or me in view. Although you take care of him when you are home, you travel so much that I feel like I have more responsibility than I want. And even when you are in town, with both of our work schedules, we don't walk Max nearly enough, which makes him more hyper.

"Bottom line is that I don't think we should keep Max and should find him another home."

Feeling relieved to get her thoughts out, she braced herself for Paul's response.

Paul collected his thoughts. "OK, what I WANT to do is tell you why you are making a big deal of nothing, but I'm going to 'play' Couch Time with you because I want to try to see Max the way you see Max, and not the way I see our great dog."

Natalie felt like the description "great dog" was a jab at her, not to mention his sarcastic phrase "play couch time," but she allowed Paul the space to continue speaking without interrupting.

"I hear that you have a problem with Max. You dislike that he has accidents inside the house and you think he is poorly behaved. You also don't like it when Max interrupts what you are doing. His barking drives you crazy. You are really mad and it seems possible you feel like I care more about Max than I do about you. Have I reflected what you are thinking and feeling?"

"Yes," Natalie replied, with a bit of surprise that Paul could state back to her what she had said to him.

At this point, Natalie and Paul have successfully started their Couch Time. Natalie clearly stated the problem and Paul reflected back to her how Max made her feel, even though his feelings were exactly opposite. Although Paul started by saying Natalie was making a "big deal out of nothing," he then steered away from his personal judgment and committed to trying to understand Natalie.

Once the opening statement by the Speaker and opening response by the Listener is achieved, then discussion of resolution can begin.

The Listener now becomes the Speaker and implements similar behavior as listed above:

- First, thank your spouse for taking the time for sharing his or her thoughts, and now taking the time to hear you.

- Remind your spouse that you love him or her and that your objective is not to win an argument, but to understand how he or she thinks and feels about the topic at hand.

- Open the conversation with your opening statement. Understandably, your preparation time will be less than your spouse's, but do use the same criteria.

- Explain to your spouse what you hope for the outcome of Couch Time.

- Throughout the conversation, try to focus on what your spouse <u>says</u> and not how their words make you <u>feel</u>. By focusing on the message and not your feelings, you have a better chance of having a productive conversation versus an emotional argument.

Back to Paul and Natalie.

> Paul started with his opening statement. "Natalie, you know I love you and I don't want the dog to be a point of conflict for us. Thank you for asking me to discuss this calmly with you, versus allowing Max to become another source of a huge argument for us.
>
> I hear and understand your anger. From my viewpoint, I love Max. He is like a part of our family and brings me so much joy. It's so fun playing ball with him in the backyard and I love taking him on jogs with me. As you know, I always had a dog growing up and it would seem so weird not to have one now. I recognize you are on the very opposite end of the spectrum, and how you feel about Max is just as important and valid as how I feel. We've got to figure out if there is a compromise in this."
>
> Natalie replied, "I agree."

At this point, Natalie and Paul have arrived at a shared understanding: the issue is to find a way to best handle taking care of the dog. How will they reach a solution?

Reaching a Resolution

Remember, on the surface, the source of conflict is not what the argument is *really* about. For instance, Natalie and Paul are discussing Max, but the underlying source of conflict is Natalie not feeling loved, appreciated or respected — and ultimately not feeling heard, understood or known. Natalie could easily say, "He doesn't *get* me! If he did, he'd know this dog is ruining my life." Reaching a resolution is all about addressing these underlying sources, and in return intimacy is created when you both feel understood.

Here are three techniques to use as you work towards reaching a resolution.

Compromise Method

Paul and Natalie's conversation started with Natalie's desire to give Max away and Paul's desire to keep him. Remember, the point of this Couch Time conversation was not to prove the worth of Max, but rather for Paul to *get* Natalie's point of view.

As Natalie and Paul continue to talk through Natalie's issues with the dog, Paul begins to realize that Natalie does not feel respected by Paul as it relates to taking care of Max. She feels she shoulders too much of the weight, and doesn't like being inconvenienced by the dog. Once Paul recognizes this, he begins to understand Natalie's point of view and can provide a productive response.

> *"Natalie, what if we looked into a way to help provide care for Max? What if we put Max in doggy daycare, or we asked a sitter to walk and feed Max before you get home? And what if I took Max to the dog-training classes we discussed a few weeks back to see if I can get him potty-trained? Would that be helpful to you?"*

By offering ways to ease her anxiety related to Max, Paul demonstrates to Natalie that he respects her point of view. As they discuss the options, they both agree that a dog-sitter and training are the next step. Natalie feels heard and understood by Paul and a compromise is reached.

But what if money was a barrier to the three solutions Paul offered? What would be another path for the Couch Time conversation?

Weight the Issue Method

One method to use when a compromise solution is not available for couples, is to Weight the Issue. Each person assigns a value — on a scale of 1 to 10 — to the importance of the issue.

Using the Weight the Issue method, Paul and Natalie's conversation might go something like this:

"Paul, thank you for the options you have suggested, but you know we can't afford any of those right now," Natalie replied.

"Well, on a scale of 1 to 10, 1 being not much, 10 being can't live with it anymore, how much does Max's behavior impact you?" Paul asked.

"A strong 8. How much does Max's behavior impact you?" Natalie asked.

"It's about a 2. I recognize that this issue has much more meaning and impact for you than it does for me. I am going to need some time to determine if I can come up with any other ideas. May I have one week to think this through and do some research to see if I can think of anything else? And would you also be willing to consider ways to find a solution?"

The quantitative score helps Paul know that this is an issue that needs to be addressed for Natalie's well-being. By weighting the issue, it is clear that Max's behavior greatly impacts Natalie, much more so than it does Paul. And ultimately, if another solution can't be found, Natalie's "8" may lead to giving Max away. But regardless of the final solution, the Weight the Issue method allows each person to understand how much the issue impacts the other. (Refer to our videocast: "Fair and Balanced Scoring" to hear more.)

Hitting a Dead End

Paul and Natalie take the week to research options to help with Max, and both come up empty-handed. Paul gets that Natalie is at a level "8" with Max, but he has no other solutions to offer. The couple may feel they've reached a dead end. At this point, however, there are two roads the couple can take.

> *"You are not what you say you are going to do; you are what you do."*

One road is "I Change Me." This method says, "I relinquish my opinion without resentment because I love my spouse more than the impact the issue has on me." In other words, although Paul loves Max, he loves Natalie more and therefore puts his wife's concerns over his own as a selfless act of love. Or conversely, Natalie recognizes that even though she is greatly bothered by Max, she doesn't want to break the bond between Max and Paul and therefore learns to adjust her thinking about Max. (Refer to our videocast: "#1 Killer of Marriage: Resentment" for more.)

Another road is to involve a third party. A trained, unbiased, third party can often help you navigate issues in ways you cannot think of yourself. A marriage counselor can help you work through the issue in a structured way. Often cost can be a barrier (or excuse) for why a couple may not seek professional help. However, marriage counseling can offer years of exponential return, making it the best investment you could make for your marriage.

Follow Through and Concluding Couch Time

By the end of the Couch Time, you should have a better understanding of your spouse, as well as ways you can help resolve the conflict. One of our favorite sayings is, "You are not what you say you are going to do; you are what you do." Actions always speak louder than words. Be sure to follow through with specific actions that show you heard and value your spouse.

For example, if Paul and Natalie agreed on Paul finding a dog-sitter and further training for Max, then it is Paul's responsibility to find the sitter and training in a timely manner and keep Natalie informed of his progress.

Once the Couch Time conversation concludes, be sure to connect with a hug and kiss. Thank each other for having the meeting and affirm each other for having a good conversation. Again, remember the 45-minute limit. If the conflict was not resolved, schedule another Couch Time to continue the conversation, if necessary.

Remember the Goal

Remember the goal of Couch Time is to *get* your spouse. Keeping this as your goal, the issues presented at Couch Time no longer serve as sources for heated arguments, but as opportunities for you and your spouse to grow closer to one another. And this is a win-win.

NEXT STEPS

- Practice Couch Time as a couple with an issue that has already been resolved in your marriage. Use something that doesn't currently cause tension or conflict so that you have the opportunity to practice the conversation.

- Once you practiced a Couch Time conversation, choose an aspect of your marriage that deserves attention. Use Couch Time to discuss that issue.

REFLECTION QUESTIONS

1. Do we feel like the frequency in which we argue is too much, too little, or just right?

2. As we reflect on our arguments, in what ways do we argue well as a couple?

3. Are there themes in our marriage we seem to continually fight about? If so, what would be the best next step for us to try to eradicate those "conflict themes" from our marriage?

4. What would it look like if we engaged in Couch Time the next time conflict arises? Are we both willing to give Couch Time a try?

5. Ask your spouse the following questions: What would it look like to you if I were truly seeking to understand you first? What do you need from me the next time conflict arises to demonstrate that I want to understand your position before I attempt to share mine?

State of the Union

*M*ark came home after a long day at work to find Cathy out of sorts. After a fairly quiet dinner, he asked, "What's wrong?" Sighing, Cathy answered, "Nothing is specifically wrong, I just feel like we are getting nowhere. I'm not mad at you, I'm just upset with where we are going. . . or if we are even going anywhere." Not completely following her train of thought, Mark just nodded. "I'm not sure I know what you mean," he said. "Help me understand."

Cathy shrugged. "Well, we can't seem to pay off the last $10,000 of college debt, which we've been struggling to do for the last two years. Thanksgiving is two weeks away, and we're going to your parents' house for lunch and spending time with my parents only in the evening . . . again. Which is exactly what we've done the last five years. We didn't even have a chance to discuss this decision because your parents asked months ago. We just repeat old holiday habits year after year.

"We've dreamed about re-landscaping the backyard since last spring but we've made no concrete decisions. Also, here we are almost at the end *of the year and we haven't even discussed if we'll be able to take a trip when we are both off from work between Christmas and New Year's."*

Once Cathy started unloading, she couldn't stop. "Again, I'm not upset with you nor blame any of this on you, it's just that with both of us working 10-hour days, by the time we get home, we are exhausted, and after dinner just want to decompress. Don't you feel like day after day it's always the same — like we're gerbils on a wheel? We never get a chance to reflect on the past or plan for the future. We're simply getting by with what's required of us, always sticking to our demanding routine."

Mark looked at Cathy with empathy, but struggled to know how to respond. Not only did he understand what she was saying, he felt the same way. How could their five-year-old marriage seem like it was already stuck in a rut?

The great news in this scenario is that Mark and Cathy did a good job communicating. Mark asked Cathy how she was feeling when he sensed something was "off." When her initial response was not clear to him, Mark demonstrated a desire to *get* his wife by asking her to explain. In her response, Cathy clearly communicated what she was feeling without assigning blame to Mark.

Nevertheless, though their communication was strong, they came upon an impasse. Mark and Cathy's gridlock was due to the fact that in their five years of marriage they had never pursued an important aspect of their relationship: strategy.

Who Has the Time?

Finding time to strategize together is a high hurdle. Consider life in terms of time. There are 168 hours in a week. When you break down a week into the hours you have together as a married couple, it's shockingly low. Most couples spend 20 waking hours together during the workweek, and anywhere from 12 to 24 waking hours together on the weekend. If you knew you only had 20 hours with your spouse this week, how would you spend it? Often, this limited amount of time is monopolized by everyday responsibilities — housework, errands, paying bills, tending to children.

As Mark and Cathy show us, if you don't strategically plan where you want your marriage to go, or what you want to accomplish, it's not going to happen on its own. Life *will* pass you by, leaving you and your spouse, and all the many hopes, dreams and good intentions you had, unfulfilled.

But it's within the planning and strategizing that you grow in *getting* your spouse — and begin understanding what is most important to him or her. Many couples want to strategize but simply don't know where to begin.

There is a solution to this all too common dilemma.

What is State of the Union?

State of the Union is the conversation tied to creating a marital strategy to help accomplish goals, hopes and dreams. Strategy, in its simplest form, reviews the past and then creates a specific plan to achieve a desired future outcome.

Like the President of the United States acknowledges and reviews the current state of the country, State of the Union is a specific time in a marriage for a couple to acknowledge and review the state of their marriage — emotionally, physically, financially and spiritually. It is a planned monthly meeting with an agenda that allows the couple to discuss the state and stability of their marriage.

The objective of State of the Union is to dedicate two hours of the month to evaluate, plan and set goals for the marriage. It is not a time to solve problems (that's Couch Time!), but a time to reflect on progress, evaluate current affairs and plan for the future. Most importantly, State of the Union is a time to discuss hopes and dreams for the marriage. Creating shared goals to reach desired results will build an unexpected intimacy — and a sense of *getting* one another.

If left unchecked, an invisible chasm can form between you and your spouse when you have goals that are not prioritized, accomplished or even shared.

> *State of the Union is the conversation tied to creating a marital strategy to help accomplish goals, hopes and dreams.*

Feelings of resentment can form — especially when there is no platform for evaluating your marriage and planning for the future.

To this end, the State of the Union conversation allows you and your spouse to discuss two important questions:

- What is the state of our marriage today?
- What steps do we need to take for the future success of our marriage?

How to Conduct a State of the Union Conversation

State of the Union is a monthly meeting that is set for a distraction-free block of time and has a planned agenda to help you move out of tactical issues and into strategic vision for the relationship.

Unlike any other *Getting Me* conversation, State of the Union requires a planned agenda. You create your agenda based on the particular topics that need the most attention. First, decide who creates the agenda and/or alternate the organizer each meeting. Because creating the agenda's talking points is a joint effort, prior to the meeting, discuss together what items need to be addressed. For the meeting to be successful, both you and your spouse must be equally committed to the topics and the importance of the meeting.

We recommend the agenda have four major topics, with subtopics under each that will be personalized by your specific focus and vision.

Here is our template for a State of the Union meeting agenda:

1. Our Relationship

- Review and discuss your relationship only. Explore how you are doing as a couple in terms of communication, intimacy, sex life, etc.

- Example questions to open this discussion might include:

    - What areas of our marriage are flourishing?

    - What areas of our marriage need attention?

    - The area of our marriage I am happiest about is . . .

    - One area of our marriage that is most frustrating to me is . . .

    - Which *Getting Me* conversations are we having well? Which conversations can be improved?

2. Our Finances

- Review and plan for your personal finances.

- Example topics might include:

    - Review of progress against household budget

    - Financial planning for upcoming large expenditures

    - Review of long-term savings goals

    - Review of giving goals (i.e., church, charity, etc.)

3. Our Family

- Discuss family issues regarding children, parents and extended family.

- Example topics might include:

  - A child's ongoing challenges in school and how you intend to address them

  - How time will be divided between families for holidays

  - New experiences you would like to individually give each child

  - How you are coping with grown children moving out of the house

4. Our Calendar

- Discuss scheduling in terms of upcoming dates and events.

- Example topics might include:

  - Ensure social commitments are booked on each others' calendars

  - Identify work commitments such as travel dates or extended work schedules that will impact others

  - Future Intentional Date Night schedule

This template should be modified to fit your needs. It is yours to add additional categories you want to strategically address each month. At minimum, we suggest the four categories above — Relationship, Finance, Family and Calendar — as a consistent part of the monthly agenda. To download the agenda, visit www.getting-me.com.

Using the template above, here is how a couple's monthly State of the Union agenda might look:

STATE OF THE UNION
FEBRUARY 20, 2017

Where is our marriage today? What are the steps for our future success?

- **OPENING PRAYER**

- **REVIEW OF NEXT STEPS FROM LAST STATE OF THE UNION**
  - Cathy
  - Mark

- **OUR RELATIONSHIP: (Cathy leads, 30 minutes)**
  - What is going great?
  - The one area I'd like to focus on in the next 30 days is...

- **OUR FINANCES: (Mark leads, 30 minutes)**
  - Review of January expenses to annual budget
  - Discussion of upcoming holiday major expenses
  - Progress towards 2017 savings goal

- **OUR FAMILY: (Cathy leads, 15 minutes)**
  - Plan for visiting relatives over spring break
  - Preparation for 7th grade teacher conferences on March 1st

- **OUR CALENDAR: (Mark leads, 15 minutes)**
  - Work events to be aware of in March
  - Begin disscussing summer vacation
  - Intentional Date Nights

- **NEXT STATE OF THE UNION MEETING: MARCH 25, 2017**
  - Our next steps

A few things to note about this agenda:

- Two overarching questions are listed at the top of each agenda to help you and your spouse remember the purpose of the meeting.

- Open the meeting in prayer. Use the first few moments of the meeting to thank God for your spouse and ask Him to give you wisdom as you discuss these aspects of your union.

- Each section of the agenda indicates which spouse will lead the other through that topic. This allows you both to be fully invested in the conversation.

- A specific amount of time is allotted for each topic. When creating the agenda, the planner needs to consider the topics on the agenda to ensure the meeting stays on time. Allotting a specific amount of time to each section increases your chance of having a productive conversation, instead of a meeting overwhelmed by the first topic on the agenda.

- "Next Steps" outlines any steps you need to take individually or collectively as a couple before the next meeting. For example, after working through the February agenda, Mark and Cathy decided their next steps would be:

    - Mark to research cost of Mexico summer vacation by next meeting.

    - Mark and Cathy to each consider amount to be given to charity in 2017.

With the agenda set, ensure each person has a copy and you are ready to conduct your first State of the Union.

The Heart of State of the Union

The heart of the State of the Union conversation is to share hopes and dreams with your spouse. To take a current status of different aspects of your marriage and discuss the future state in each area, while having complete freedom to strategize about what you hope for your marriage in the days to come.

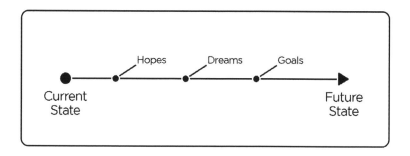

When was the last time you and your spouse sat down and articulated your hopes and dreams to one another — and then put pen to paper with a plan for how and when it would be accomplished? Even those with the best of intentions may decide to have a debt paid off

> *When was the last time you and your spouse sat down and articulated your hopes and dreams to one another?*

within the year or have their porch re-painted before summer, only to see their great ideas drift away. Follow-through is where most couples find themselves stuck and frustrated with one another, projecting feelings of never being heard or even loved.

 State of the Union is not a time to resolve conflict. (If conflict arises, agree to a *Couch Time* to discuss that issue.) For example, if you come to a disagreement over finances that can't be resolved in five minutes or less, table it. The goal is to avoid conflict that derails the momentum of your strategic meeting. (Refer to our videocast: "When Conflict Arises in State of the Union" for more.)

Remember to always return to the heart of State of the Union. It's a conversation to create a strategy for hopes, dreams and goals with your spouse. The more you are on the same page, the more connected and unified you will become as you pursue common goals, proving that you really *get* one another.

What Makes State of the Union Successful?

The State of the Union meeting is the conversation most likely to be placed on the backburner. Couples decide on a date for this meeting and then life happens — a child has a rescheduled sports game for the same time as the meeting, or a work commitment pops up for the night that was chosen to meet. When something gets in the way the couple quickly says, "Since we can't meet, let's just wait until next

> *The heart of the State of the Union conversation is to find unity with your spouse.*

month." When the couple finds themselves with yet another conflict the next month, they cancel the meeting again. As Gregg often says to couples, "Great excuse, bad choice."

Commitment to meeting on a regular and continual basis is key to the success of this conversation. When a couple is participating in this conversation on a regular and continual basis, they are making intentional plans and decisions for the future state of the marriage. It becomes more difficult to track progress or discuss new topics if the meetings are intermittent and not prioritized.

How to Exit State of the Union

After a State of the Union conversation, be sure to thank your spouse for the time he or she gave to the conversation and planning for the future. Ensure each person is clear on his or her individual responsibilities before the next meeting. Confirm the meeting date of the next State of the Union.

The Unexpected Benefit of State of the Union

Most couples don't realize the benefit of attending to the business aspects of marriage is intimacy. How can planning and intimacy possibly be connected?

Perhaps the most memorable explanation of intimacy is this: *you get me*. When we allow another person to really "see" inside of us, a closeness develops. When we share hopes, goals and dreams with another person, we allow them into a place and space that is not open for all.

Couples will find that spending two hours a month sharing hopes and dreams for their marriage draws them closer to one another. With so many day-to-day conversations based on everyday problem solving and responsibilities, State of the Union allows a couple to reflect on dreams that have turned into plans and to celebrate progress. Some couples keep a notebook of their State of the Union agendas as a journal of how the marriage has grown and evolved over the year. It's inspiring to look back on! Dreaming about the future opens up an excitement for things to come and, in turn, will pull you closer together as you plan and work toward those goals.

> *Perhaps the most memorable explanation of intimacy is this:* **you get me**.

Remember the Goal

Strategizing with your spouse may not sound romantic, but the purpose behind it is. Remember the goal of State of the Union is to *get* one another by creating a strategy for your marriage that helps you accomplish goals, hopes and dreams. In acknowledging the current state of your marriage and implementing a plan for a desired future state, a natural appreciation for one another will surface as you prioritize important aspects of your marriage. In seeking to understand your spouse's goals, hopes and dreams you will grow in *getting* one another more intimately.

NEXT STEPS

- Test our theory! Track how much time you spend together as a couple in waking hours during one week. This number should only affirm the need for State of the Union conversations.

- Determine the date and time for your first State of the Union meeting and who will create the meeting agenda. You can find a template for the meeting agenda at www.getting-me.com.

- After three months, evaluate how this conversation is moving your marriage toward achieving goals you have set for the future. This might even be a great agenda topic for your fourth State of the Union.

REFLECTION QUESTIONS

1. How many hours a week are we able to think about the state of our marriage?

2. How would our marriage benefit from having a dedicated time to take a status check and plan for the future?

3. What will get in the way of our having this conversation on a regular basis? How can we proactively address that hurdle?

4. Who would be better at creating the monthly agenda? Is the spouse who might be better at creating the agenda fine with doing so? Or should we alternate?

5. How do we want to modify the State of the Union meeting agenda to be ours?

Pillow Talk

*I*t was 10:00 p.m., the kids were down and the house was locked for the night. Unusually, Scott and Susan were both headed to the bedroom at the same time, as neither chose to deal with emails unanswered from the day nor the kids' toys scattered on the living room floor. Scott took the mutual move to the bedroom as a sign that Susan was feeling amorous. As he looked at her slyly, Scott said with a playful tone, "How about a little action tonight?" Little did he know the floodgate that his question was about to open.

"Are you kidding?" exclaimed Susan. "Didn't you even notice that I couldn't clean up the kids' toys since I am so dog-tired? You clearly didn't have the day I had. The kids were acting crazy all day and literally wore out my last nerve. And truly, you think it's a turn-on for me when you say so stupidly 'how about a little action?' That is so totally not romantic. Actually, tonight I find it repulsive."

Scott just looked at her, suddenly feeling embarrassed by his playfulness.

Susan continued. "And not only am I exhausted, we still have yet to discuss how we are going to handle my car needing repair. Are you taking the car to the mechanic in the morning or do we need to meet midday at the repair shop?"

"I don't know," Scott replied. "Can we just figure that out in the morning?"

"So, let me get this straight," Susan sneered. "You have enough energy to stay up and have sex, but you don't have enough energy to discuss how we are getting the car to the repair shop? So typical."

"What do you mean 'typical'?" Scott snapped back.

"Never mind," Susan muttered, making her way to the bathroom to wash her face.

Scott got into bed and within ten minutes was fast asleep. After washing her face, Susan got into bed and laid awake for an hour reflecting on her overwhelming day. She worried about the car needing repair, which led to her worrying about finances, which led to worrying about her marriage. How could he sleep at a time like this?

Have you and your spouse ever had a "Scott and Susan moment"? Where miscommunication surrounding sex has turned an opportunity for intimacy into a moment of conflict and tension? For many, feelings of sad, mad or fear surface around the topic of sex. Even the moments intended for fun can turn into feelings of anger.

Why is talking to your spouse about sex so difficult?

Let's Talk About Sex

Perhaps the difficult nature of talking about sex stems back to when your parents first forced an awkward conversation with you about the birds and the bees. Or when you sat among your peers blushing as your health teacher discussed the anatomy of sex. These attempts to explain such a physically and emotionally complex part of life left many of us still wondering: how do we "do" sex?

Then as we got older and well into our marriages, it became clear that no one taught us *how* to talk about sex with our spouse.

Since we bring different histories and experiences into the bedroom, it can be daunting to discuss such an intimate topic. How many of you have something you wish you could share with your spouse regarding your sex life, but have chosen to keep it to yourself? Perhaps you feel embarrassed, or afraid, or unprepared to hear how your spouse may respond.

> *How many of you have something you wish you could share with your spouse regarding your sex life, but have chosen to keep it to yourself?*

But what if talking about sex didn't have to be so complicated or nerve-wracking? What if Pillow Talk became an opportunity for you to *get* your spouse — and his or her needs — so that your sex life became more enjoyable for you both?

What is Pillow Talk?

Pillow Talk is a series of sexually-focused conversations — both In Bed and Out of Bed — that help create an opportunity for you to *get* one another's specific preferences surrounding your sex life. Out of Bed conversations help define your specific sexual preferences while you are not *in the moment*, and are positive in nature or at least neutral in tone. In Bed conversations revolve around the art of lovemaking while you are *in the moment* and are positive or instructive, not critical or blaming.

Before we begin, we need to present a foundational concept (that may have you questioning us at first!). Our intention in presenting this concept however, is to help you and your spouse reach a shared understanding of the deeper motivation behind a man wanting to have sex with his wife. Even if you disagree, your willingness to understand its significance will not only help you *get* your spouse, but may also encourage more emotional and physical connection.

Sex is Not a "Need"

Yes, we can hear the collective groan of most men as they read that. Certainly when a man feels a sexual urge, he *needs* to have sex. Right? We disagree.

We do agree that men have sexual desires that cause a need. The actual physical need, however, is not for sex — but for ejaculation. As Gregg often says, "an orgasm is an orgasm is an orgasm." Whether a man ejaculates during sex with his wife or because of masturbation, the physical, bodily response is exactly the same. However, the emotional response — ejaculation with someone he loves versus ejaculation by himself — is completely different.

 In Gregg's practice, he has asked countless husbands and wives: "For the remaining nights of your marriage, if you could *only* have physical, non-sexual touch (such as cuddling, hand holding, back rubs) OR sexual intercourse with *no* non-sexual touch (as in, intercourse with no affection), which would you choose?" The overwhelming response is couples choose physical, non-sexual but affectionate touch over intercourse because ultimately both husband and wife want to feel intimately connected. (See our videocast: "Which Would You Choose?" to hear more.)

Why does this matter? For many, when a husband, like Scott, asks his wife for *"a little action tonight"* it can be perceived by the wife as selfish or self-serving. Like Susan's *"Are you kidding?"* response, all you may really want is your husband to *get* that you had a long day. But, with this new understanding that sex is not a need, your husband wants you to *get* that he simply wants to connect with you. He *could* meet the physical need of ejaculation on his own, but he *wants* to satisfy his physical need by feeling emotionally connected to the one he loves the most. Ultimately, it should be reassuring that you both want the same thing: emotional connection.

Now, knowing the sexual experience is a point of emotional connection for both you and your spouse — not just a physical one — let's first look at how you can clarify your preferences during the Out of Bed conversations of Pillow Talk. The better your spouse understands your preferences, the more you will feel your spouse *gets* what you want from your sex life.

Pillow Talk: Out of Bed

Out of Bed conversations are centered around your sex life but are had outside the bedroom. As mentioned earlier, these conversations help define preferences and are positive in nature or at least neutral in tone. By addressing bedtime routines and sexual preferences outside of the bedroom, you are likely to speak more freely and with less emotion. Your goal is to *get* your spouse and his or her preferences in the bedroom.

Out of Bed: Harmonizing Bedtime Routines

 As Scott and Lisa showed us, sex and bedtime can be especially tricky. For starters, couples rarely go to bed at the *exact* same time. And when they do, each person prepares for sleep differently. One may fall asleep immediately, while the other needs a routine to wind down. One may read, while the other watches TV or reviews social media. To this point, we believe the bed has two purposes *only* — for sleeping and for sex — not for TV or technology! (Refer to our videocast: "A Bed for Two" for more.)

Bedtime is also when anxiety tends to kick in. The rise of fatigue and the release of daily responsibilities can cause the brain's worries and concerns to surface. Because of this, many marital arguments occur at bedtime. Instead of self-soothing, one spouse feels compelled to dump anxiety on the other. "Now I lay me down to sleep" quickly turns into "now I lay my anxiety on you!"

Bedtime can also be tricky when couples approach the bedroom with different agendas in mind — one wanting sex and one wanting sleep. This conflict of interest can create a disappointing end to the day for one or both of you.

Harmonizing your bedtime routines, even if you don't go to bed at the same time, can decrease disappointment at the end of the day. As discussed in Comings and Goings, couples should connect at bedtime in a non-sexual way.

At bedtime, it is the <u>first</u> person going to bed that has the responsibility of connecting with his or her spouse to end the day. This ritual can be defined by the couple, but should include at least two elements: a positive, verbal exchange and a physical, non-sexual touch. For instance, your ritual could be:

- Tell your spouse you are going to bed, share an affirming comment ("I am blessed to be married to you!") and exchange a kiss

- Ten minutes before bedtime, ask your spouse about the best part of their day, then ask how you can pray for him or her tomorrow, and share a hug

- Pray together and exchange a kiss

By creating a non-sexual bedtime ritual, it allows you to end the day connecting with one another. Then each person can fall asleep in their own pattern.

A great Intentional Date Night topic is to discuss how you like to go to bed as a couple. Take the time to ask your spouse the following questions:

- Is it important to you if we go to bed at the same time? Why or why not?

- If I go to bed before you do, what are some things I can do to show my love and appreciation for you at the end of the day?

- Do you mind if my bedtime ritual is independent of yours — like reading a book? Or would you rather us have a dependent activity like cuddling?

- Would you be open to praying together at bedtime even if one of us is going to bed before the other?

- Do you expect us to have sex when we go to bed at the same time?

As we mentioned earlier, if you have something weighing heavily on your mind, bedtime is *not* the time to initiate a challenging discussion. Because both of you are tired from the day's events, it is better to exercise self-control and wait to discuss the issue. How many of us can fall asleep soundly after a heated bedtime argument? If you have a troubling issue you want to discuss, schedule a Couch Time before you go to bed. Then you can end the day with the comfort that a time and place have been arranged to dive into the issue.

Harmonizing your bedtime routine is a way to ensure connection at the end of the day. But what about when you want more than a hug or kiss? With so many variables personally impacting you both, it's important to share your specific preferences with one another. This Out of Bed conversation focuses on your spouse's perspective and preferences — from how often he or she wants sex to any new positions he or she would like (or not like) to try.

CONVERSATION 5 — PILLOW TALK

Out of Bed: Your Spouse's Perspective

The best time to discuss your sexual relationship with your spouse is while you are fully clothed and away from the bedroom. You may think you know your spouse's answers, but a conversation centered on clarifying questions may enlighten you both. Set aside a specific Out of Bed time to ask one another:

- Ideally, how often would you like to have sex?

- Do you see our bed as a place only for sleep or for both sleep and sex?

- Are you open to having sex in other places than our bed? If so, where is your favorite place to have sex? Or is there a new place you would like to try?

- What do you like when we have sex? Anything you don't like or is off-limits for you?

- Is there a new position you would like to try?

- Do you like to have sex with the lights on or off?

- How long do you think a sexual experience should last — from foreplay to intercourse to after?

- If you are not in the mood to have sex when I ask, how can we find another time to have sex?

- What can I do to create an environment to make engaging in sex easy for you?

- What can I do to help make sex more comfortable or more enjoyable for you?

If any answers pose a conflict, then commit to a Couch Time for further discussion. As an example, *frequency* is a shared conflict for so many, we thought we would demonstrate how a Couch Time might unfold around the topic.

The conflict: *Tim wants to have sex three times a week, while Sally wants to have sex once a week.*

Step 1:   Preparation

- Instead of lashing out, Tim stays calm and determines what he wants the end result of the conversation to be.

  Tim's goal is not to win, but to communicate about the issue in such a way that Sally *gets* him and a compromise is reached. He should consider how to explain the issue so that Sally can see it from his point of view. He should also consider what kinds of questions he could ask Sally to better understand her point of view.

- Tim is aware of the tone and nonverbals he will use during the conversation.

  Good communication takes into account more than words. If Tim rolls his eyes, crosses his arms, or turns away from Sally, she will sense his disapproval. Instead, Tim knows to face Sally, make eye contact, and resist showing nonverbal disagreement with his face or body.

  - Tim creates an opening statement and practices the tone and way in which he will present it.

  "Sally, I would like to share with you why having sex at least three times a week is important to me so that you can understand where I am coming from."

Step 2:   Arrangement

- Tim and Sally agree on a specific time and place for their Couch Time.

The place should be a private location, where Tim and Sally can look at each other eye to eye, and be in such close proximity they have the ability to touch.

Step 3:   Conversation

Using the guidelines in Couch Time, Tim explains to Sally his need for a higher frequency in having sex. Sally should not put down or deny Tim's need, but rather listen in such a way that she suspends her own needs to truly *get* his perspective.

Once Sally feels that she has heard Tim, the roles reverse. Sally explains to Tim why her need for sex is less frequent, and Tim listens to understand.

Once Tim and Sally have heard each other's reasoning for their desired frequency for sex, they might discuss the following:

- Is there a compromise we can reach in terms of frequency?
- What roadblocks exist that are preventing us from reaching this compromise? How can we overcome them?
- Can we commit to this frequency for one month and discuss the results after the month is over?
- What can we each do for the other to meet this compromise?
- Will we have sex in a planned or spontaneous way?

Using Couch Time for conversations that impact your sex life allows you to discuss critical aspects of your marriage without the pressure of being in a sexual moment.

At times, issues around sex seem unresolvable and the help of a licensed professional therapist may be needed. This could include situations such as:

- A compromise on frequency of sex can't be reached, despite several conversations

- One partner wants to engage in unhealthy sexual activities

- Past physical, emotional or sexual abuse have been experienced by one partner

- Emotional or physical pain is present when engaged in sexual activity

The involvement of a professional third party in these conversations can serve as a helpful investment in your marriage, when you sense you cannot discuss the issue any further on your own.

Out of Bed: Planned Versus Spontaneous

Most couples think that to have great sex, it has to be spontaneous. This is one of the biggest myths about sex in a marriage. Spontaneous is defined as *"occurring as a result of a sudden inner impulse or inclination and without premeditation or external stimulus."* Think how difficult it is to do *anything* spontaneously as a couple, and especially when you are married with kids!

When one spouse is unexpectedly *in the mood* and the other is not, conflict typically occurs. The one who is *in the mood* feels rejected and the other feels guilty for not wanting to engage. Don't misunderstand us, spontaneous lovemaking is a wonderful gift when those impromptu moments arise. However, how often do both you and your spouse want to have sex at the exact same time?

The healthiest way to keep sex a priority in your marriage is to have a plan. Planning can decrease the anxiety of the unknown and increase the odds of engaging in sex on a regular basis. Perhaps it's a standing night each week or looking week to week for the best time to connect. Many people reject the concept of planning for sex, but having a plan doesn't take away from the experience once you start connecting. It does, however, ensure you make the time to do so.

Preparing for Sex

Regardless of whether planned or spontaneous, sex often starts 24 hours before intercourse begins. Typically, women are more inclined to have sex when they feel emotionally connected with their spouse beforehand. Conversely, men feel more emotionally con-nected to their wives after intercourse. With this in mind, both husbands and wives can take into consideration what could help prepare one another for a meaningful sexual experience.

> *The best time to discuss your sexual relationship with your spouse is while you are fully clothed and away from the bedroom.*

A Word to the Husbands

Husbands, you can create opportunities for connection by put-ting forth extra effort the day before. Remember what we learned from Scott and Susan? A pithy *"how about a little action tonight"* two minutes beforehand doesn't do the trick. The day before you want to engage, keep at the forefront of your mind that your wife may feel more inclined towards sex when she feels emotionally connected with you. Therefore, you could:

- Engage in thought-provoking conversation, to show genuine interest in how she is feeling or what she is thinking.

- Help around the house without being asked. Demonstrate you care by your actions. For instance, make dinner, remove the dishes from the dishwasher or put away the folded laundry.

- Reflect on your wife throughout your years of dating and marriage: what does it look like when you know your wife feels connected with you? Work toward that.

Be very conscientious that sexual physical touch does not automatically "flip a switch" for your wife. If she is standing at the kitchen sink or sitting at her desk, coming up and rubbing her shoulders can be a nice way to connect in a physical, non-sexual way. However, immediately moving from a shoulder rub to grabbing her breasts does not make her feel emotionally connected to you.

Consider establishing bedtime rituals that are not sexual to create connection. Would she be open to cuddling for five minutes before falling asleep? Or might she be interested in a prolonged kissing session with no expectation of sex to follow? Perhaps a ten-minute massage is all she needs to know you care.

A Word to the Wives

Your husband may require little preparation before engaging in sex. In fact, your eyes could simply glance toward the bed and he would be ready to go! And yet, he still wants to feel pursued. He needs to know you're attracted to him and that you want to have sex with him — that you're not just accommodating him. Keeping this in mind, remember to pursue your husband in ways that you know he would like. Therefore, you could:

- Create a romantic setting that shows him you are ready to engage.
- Be the one who initiates sexual connection.
- Enthusiastically show him you enjoy engaging in sex with him.

And who knows? You might take more pleasure than you expected in being the instigator!

A Word to You Both

There are exceptions to every rule. Some wives prefer sex more than their husbands. Some husbands need extra TLC before engaging, and wouldn't appreciate his wife pouncing on him. Whatever works for your marriage is what works best. The most important point is to communicate your preferences so that you *get* one another.

Pillow Talk: In Bed

Whether you are on an Intentional Date Night, a scheduled Couch Time, or an impromptu discussion over coffee, sharing your sexual desires and preferences are likely to come more easily with your clothes on. It's when your clothes are off and sex is taking place that the In Bed conversation begins.

In Bed: Conversation During Sexual Intimacy

When your spouse is naked in front of you, it doesn't seem like a natural time to talk, does it? This moment can be such a physically vulnerable time that we inadvertently put our guard up so we are not hurt. For this reason, couples tend to shy away from talking while having sex. However, talking during sex and giving your spouse instructive feedback as to what you like will create a stronger sense of connection.

Generally speaking, conversation during sex can revolve around two topics:

- What makes your spouse feel connected?
- What is pleasurable for your spouse?

- Don't be afraid to talk about what makes your spouse feel connected during sex.

- Is it looking into each other's eyes?

- Is it certain types of language?

- Is it certain aspects of the environment — lights on or off? Music? Scents?

- Be willing to ask "is this the right place?" or "should I try this?"

Be confident in asking questions to help you understand what is best for him or her. Knowing the answers can help you navigate the moment of intimacy in a truly pleasing way.

The only rule? Talking during sex must be positive. Negative comments can generate feelings of shame for your spouse.

Also, don't be afraid to laugh together while having sex. Having fun and enjoying the moment allows your spouse to see you vulnerably and authentically. Engaging in sex with your spouse should be an enjoyable time.

Remember the Goal

Remember the goal of Pillow Talk is to *get* your spouse. By understanding his or her sexual preferences, you will start to understand his or her most intimate side. Pillow Talk allows you to bring to light the hidden intricacies of what makes sex most pleasurable for you. There is no age limit or season of life where connecting intimately with your spouse loses its value. Sex is a continual experience which can only increase in richness, as your marriage evolves and you grow in *getting* one another.

NEXT STEPS

- Set aside a time for Pillow Talk: Out of Bed. Start the discussion using the questions throughout the chapter to learn your spouse's preferences.

- Schedule a Couch Time to discuss any unresolved issues within your sex life. Use the Couch Time model to understand your spouse — not win him or her over.

- Individually, go through the questions presented in the chapter and answer each one honestly before you discuss with your spouse.

REFLECTION QUESTIONS

1. Are you comfortable sharing with one another your preferences for sex — both In Bed and Out of Bed? What can you do to increase that comfort?

2. Does anything need to be addressed within your marriage or outside your marriage that impacts your level of sexual intimacy together? How will you address these issues?

3. What has worked best for your marriage — planned or spontaneous sex? Answer this question openly and honestly, and share with your spouse.

4. If you could describe your ideal sex life with your spouse — what would it look like?

Sacred Time

*A*ll through her teenage years, Kathryn never allowed herself to believe *that "love at first sight" was a realistic way to start a relationship. But after college she met Kyle, and her mind quickly changed.*

Kyle was handsome and friendly, without a pretentious air. Kathryn was beautiful and outgoing, and one to never know a stranger. Their story is one fairytales are made of. The two literally met across a crowded room at the wedding of a mutual friend. Their shared smiles and nods 'hello' quickly turned into an invitation onto the dance floor. After a few glasses of wine and a fantastic time dancing, Kyle summoned the courage to ask Kathryn for her phone number. Two weeks later, they found themselves at a baseball game and dinner.

The baseball game turned out to be a great way to break the ice. Kathryn loved Kyle's humor and how attentive he was to her. Kyle thought Kathryn was a great sport when she did not complain about the heat or the obstructed view from their stadium seats. The ease of being in each other's company flowed into an electric conversation at dinner. Kathryn could barely hold her excitement as she asked Kyle question after question, eager to learn more about him. Kyle was flattered that she had such interest in him, and felt completely at ease with her. At the end of the evening, Kyle said, "I usually don't do this, but can I go ahead and ask you out for a second date?" Kathryn said "yes!", they kissed and at that moment, they both fell in love.

After two years of dating, and a Hollywood-style wedding, their story personified "love at first sight." Yet four months into their marriage, the couple experienced a notable shift that shook Kathryn to the core.

Kathryn's job required her to travel throughout the week; Kyle's did not. Coming home late from work on Friday nights, the newlywed bride was dismayed at the condition she found the house in week after week. Dirty laundry and a sink full of dishes greeted her before Kyle had the opportunity to say "hello."

One evening, Kathryn and Kyle were talking on the phone, miles apart due to work. Since Kathryn would be home the next day, she asked Kyle if he could throw a load of towels in the wash before she returned. "I'll try," he answered. His response made Kathryn furious. Not one to hold back, she unloaded on Kyle like she never had before. Kyle sat on the other end of the line in silence. His silence only infuriated her more. In a rage, she slammed down the phone and burst into tears, alone in her hotel room. And all because of dirty towels — or so it seemed.

The anger she felt toward him made her wonder, "Did I just make the biggest mistake of my life? . . . Do I not love him anymore?" And just like that she remembered her "wisdom" of her youth: there is no such thing as "love at first sight." The one she found so attentive at the baseball game, now could not manage a simple household chore. "Does he even love me anymore?" she wondered.

What Happens When Love Changes?

Every married couple hits a point in their marriage where they sense that their love has changed. (You are not alone.) And there's good reason why every couple finds themselves at this place.

There is no denying there was a very strong attraction when you first met your spouse. This is what some call "love at first sight." But, we propose your initial attraction was not love, but chemicals and hormones "firing off" in your body. Research has proven that due to a mix of hormones and chemicals — namely testosterone, estrogen, adrenaline, dopamine and serotonin — you experience an intense rush of pleasure when you are together, or even just thinking about that "special someone." Often described as "a feeling I've never had before," these hormones and chemicals, in actuality, make us feel like we are in love. But, this mix of chemicals is not enough to withstand the test of time. So, what happens once you are in a committed relationship? Typically, that feeling begins to take a different shape, just like it did for Kathryn, and couples then start to question whether or not their initial feeling for the other was really love.

Because we allow culture to help write our definition of love, we are greatly impacted by the messages presented to us. We allow movies — like Jerry Maguire (*you complete me*), and music — like The Beatles (*all you need is love*), and books — like 50 Shades of Grey (*unhealthy lust equals love*) to shape what love should look like. We also look to other couples for comparison — your sister and brother-in-law who go on a date every week, or your neighbor whose husband starts her car for her to warm it up on cold mornings. With these one-sided takes on love, we then put a lot of pressure — spoken and unspoken — on our spouse to fulfill what we believe love is. This flimsy foundation for defining love, coupled with expecting our spouse to be the one who satisfies us completely, is often the first step toward disillusionment — which, if left unchecked, can lead to divorce.

From the moment you met your spouse and started dating, what if your definition of love was incomplete, or worse, incorrect? Is it too late to find a true, unchanging definition for love?

A New Definition for Love

We believe it's not too late. There is a kind of love that never changes — a love that can fill you in such a unique way that you can love your spouse better than you are loving him or her today. But before we share this new definition, let's look at the current dynamic of love in your marriage.

Love for most married couples looks like this:

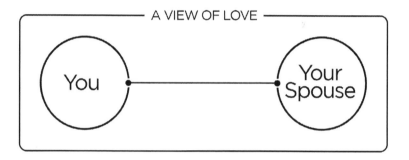

Notice here, the love you have for your spouse is linear. Seems simple enough, right? Just you and your spouse, connected and in love. This view of love might work when circumstances are good in your life: your job is going well, you feel well, and you have enough money in the bank. When life is easy, it is easy to love well. This linear kind of love also assumes that your spouse will always be capable of giving back the same kind of love he or she originally gave when you first met. When she pursues you as enthusiastically as she did when

> *When life is easy, it is easy to love well.*

you first started dating, you can love. When he pays you a compliment or does a chore around the house without you asking first, you can love.

> *When life is hard, it is hard to love well.*

Yet, over time, love starts to look different — especially if you define love based on your own ability. With this linear kind of love, you can only give away what you have to give. When the job gets tough, you are sleep deprived, or the bills pile up, love begins to run dry. When life is hard, it is hard to love well. Who can be loving when the stresses of life are attacking? Because this common view of love is based on each person's ability, the feelings between a couple change as life circumstances change and as each person evolves.

The longer the couple has been married, the more the original view of love is challenged. When love seems to change, couples begin to ask *what happened to the person I married?* Often, Gregg will hear a client say, "I love [my spouse], I'm just not IN love any-

> *The longer the couple has been married, the more the original view of love is challenged.*

more." This linear view of love ultimately leads to a dead end. Especially when one spouse expects the other to change back into the person he or she first loved.

What happens then? Statistically, this is when couples conclude that they don't love one another anymore, and often entertain ideas of separation. But what if instead, couples worked together to redefine love and started to explore the possibilities for what true love is?

The Love Triangle: A Strong Foundation

Before you get the wrong impression about our suggesting your marriage needs a "love triangle," it's not what you think! To build a strong foundation for a healthy marriage, a straight line will never be enough — your marriage needs a "love triangle." Like a triangle, a marriage should have a strong foundation with two sides reaching upward *and* toward each other. And most important to *this* triangle, there needs to be three people actively involved in your marriage: you, your spouse and God.

The Love Triangle is based on four Scriptures that show how we should relate to one another in marriage (our most important earthly relationship) and will begin to help us create a concrete, biblical definition for love — one that is secure and unchanging. First, let us present each Scripture with a simple explanation. Then, we will apply these four Scriptures to your marriage.

> *To build a strong foundation for a healthy marriage, a straight line will never be enough — your marriage needs a "love triangle."*

Matthew 22:35-38	The Great Commandment
John 13:34-35	The New Commandment
1 Corinthians 13:4-8	A Biblical Definition of Love
Genesis 2:20b-24	Definition of Biblical Marriage

Matthew 22:35-38 (NIV):   The Great Commandment

One of them, an expert in the law, tested him with this question: "Teacher, which is the greatest commandment in the Law?" Jesus replied: "'Love the

Lord your God with all your heart and with all your soul and with all your mind.' This is the first and greatest commandment."

In the context of marriage, these verses imply **our primary relationship is with God**. We are called to love God in an "all in" kind of way: with our heart, soul and mind. (Refer to our videocast: "Loving God All In" for more.)

John 13:34-35 (NIV):   The New Commandment

"A new command I give you: Love one another. As I [Jesus] have loved you, so you must love one another. By this everyone will know you are my disciples, if you love one another."

If you had to answer in two or three words, *how* does Christ love you, what would those words be? Perhaps faithfully, sacrificially, and entirely? (Or pragmatically, accusingly, and half-heartedly? We hope not.) We are called to love those in our lives as Christ loves us. Note that this is the new "commandment", not the new "suggestion."

1 Corinthians 13:4-8 (NIV):   A Biblical Definition of Love

Love is patient, love is kind. It does not envy, it does not boast, it is not proud. It does not dishonor others, it is not self-seeking, it is not easily angered, it keeps no record of wrongs. Love does not delight in evil but rejoices with the truth. It always protects, always trusts, always hopes, always perseveres.

Take a second and count how many descriptions for the word *love* you can find in this verse. Based on our count, there are at least 15 active descriptions for biblical love. The Apostle Paul is turning our culture's description of love upside down. Love is not about fulfilling your own needs; love is active, serving, and selfless.

But again, can *anyone* love like this? This definition of love seems utterly impossible to enact. Stay with us.

Genesis 2:20b-24 (NIV): Definition of Biblical Marriage

But for Adam no suitable helper was found. So the Lord God caused the man to fall into a deep sleep; and while he was sleeping, he took one of the man's ribs and then closed up the place with flesh. Then the Lord God made a woman from the rib he had taken out of the man, and he brought her to the man. The man said, "This is now bone of my bones and flesh of my flesh; she shall be called 'woman,' for she was taken out of man." That is why a man leaves his father and mother and is united to his wife, and they become one flesh.

God ordained marriage between man and wife so they would become *one flesh*. In essence, this scripture is the very first definition of marriage — the act of a man and woman leaving their own individual lives to cling to one another. The phrase *one flesh* can take a lifetime to fully understand, but, for our purposes, let's draw an analogy to a team. Think of your favorite sports team — where many players make up one collective unit. When one person on the team does well, the team celebrates. When one person on the team makes a mistake, a successful team doesn't get paralyzed by the error, but rather attempts to encourage each other and move forward.

These words *one flesh* means you and your spouse are one. So much so, that when your spouse is hurt, you are hurt — or even when you hurt your spouse, you've hurt yourself, too. Marriage calls us to create our own team — to celebrate the great moments of life and to stay side by side when life is challenging — and even when our spouse fails us.

Restructuring the Definition of Love

So, how can understanding these verses transform your most important earthly relationship? What is it about each verse that reveals your need to strengthen the way you love your spouse? The big epiphany we want you to understand is: *to love your spouse the way the Bible defines love, your spouse can't be #1.* Let's recall each verse's significance as it relates to you in your marriage.

- **Matthew 22:35-38 — The Great Commandment — *Love God first.*** Your primary relationship is not with your spouse, but with God. Marriages thrive most when both the husband and the wife are loving God "all in."

- **John 13:34-35 — The New Commandment — *Love like Christ.*** You are called to love your spouse in the same way Christ loved you. How would you prefer your spouse describe the way <u>you</u> love him or her? Can you see how loving your spouse like Christ will look more like a deep and meaningful way to love? For many of us, we wonder how we could ever love like Christ. Hold on to that thought as we continue.

- **1 Corinthians 13:4-8 — A Biblical Definition of Love — *Love selflessly.*** Love is not passive. Love is active, serving, and selfless. The biblical definition of love is very different than a worldly definition of love.

- **Genesis 2:20b-24 — Definition of Biblical Marriage — *Become one flesh.*** Man and woman are to become *one flesh*, establishing their own union, becoming a team.

What happens when we remove God from the equation and place ourselves first? This re-positioning disrupts what God intended for our marriages.

By putting God first, your ability to love others — especially your spouse — becomes easier as you surrender to God and not to your emotions. God then gives you a daily, fresh source of love to give your spouse; no longer is it dependent only on you. This changes the model of marriage. We cease our chasing after a cultural definition and now have an infinite source of love coming from the One who defined it.

God has brought you someone to love in the same way that Christ loves you. It may seem counterintuitive, but by putting God before your spouse, you will love your spouse like never before.

The Love Triangle model for marriage looks like:

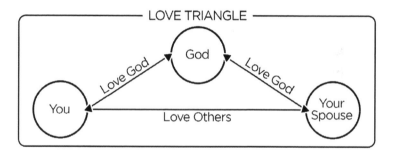

The Love Triangle provides three new elements to your marriage:

1. **Your focus is on loving God first.** The arrowheads suggest a continual call for you to connect to God and a limitless source of love and support flows from God to you.

2. **Your spouse's focus is on loving God first.** Again, the arrowheads of the line represent a continuous effort and a well-spring of love from a source that is not you.

3. **Your ability to love one another well grows exponentially.** When you and your spouse both put God first, you have an infinite ability to love each other well. Love no longer depends on worldly standards or your own ability, but on a direct manifestation of how you love God.

With this new structure in mind, we urge you to reconsider how you define love in your marriage. Instead of relying on your own interpretation, try defining love as an action fueled by your primary relationship with God. If you agree with this concept, but your spouse does not, there is still hope for transforming your marriage into this triangle. (Refer to our videocast: "Creating a Love Triangle" for more.)

With a newfound biblical definition of love, you are better prepared to grow closer together spiritually. But how do you do this? How do you put God first before your spouse, your kids or even yourself?

Sacred Time: Building a Collective Relationship with God

To love well, in the very best way you can, you need to forget about your spouse for a minute and focus on your primary relationship: with God. The more time you invest in loving God, the more naturally love will flow into your marriage. The healthiest marriage is the one in which *both* spouses are investing in God as their primary relationship. The great news is this investment can be made individually — yet discussed and explored together as a couple in Sacred Time.

Sacred Time is time a married couple spends together growing individually and collectively with God. This time is devoted to engaging in four spiritual disciplines and sacred conversations: prayer, worship, study, and confession. Though there are many spiritual disciplines — we feel these four will drive sacred conversations and spiritual intimacy with the Lord.

As you read about how to partake in each sacred conversation, please don't allow it to overwhelm you. If this is your first time pursuing spiritual disciplines and sacred conversations, we have provided easy entry points for you and your spouse. It takes time to build each discipline and works best if you commit to one discipline at a time. Then, as that discipline becomes a habit, move to another. Regardless of the discipline you choose, we are confident you will see an impact in your marriage as you both commit to growing collectively with God.

Sacred Time: Worship

For many couples, attendance at a Sunday morning worship service can fluctuate based on convenience, or who is preaching that morning, or whether or not you have a new ensemble you want to wear.

But, worship can be one of the best times for a couple to grow in their relationship with God. If your lens of worship is focused on meeting with God, time spent together in a worship service can be transformative. As a couple, this transformative time can serve as a weekly "team meeting" with God, to intentionally and purposefully connect together with Him.

How to develop the spiritual discipline of Worship:

- **Commit to worship weekly**. Don't let church be a last-minute Sunday morning decision. Decide that worship is part of your weekly routine because you need time with the Lord for the week ahead. If you are out of town, remember some of the best worship moments can be in nature, with a Bible and a heart seeking the Lord.

- **Be an active participant.** As tempting as it is to make the grocery list during the worship service, focus your mind on the message. Take notes of key points, or close your eyes during hymns and allow the collective singing to resonate in your ears and in your heart.

The Sacred Worship Conversation

After the service, discuss how worship impacted you. On the way home from church or over lunch, share your takeaway from the sermon and how it will impact you for the week. Be careful to not use the worship service as an indictment on your spouse. The spouse who says (or even just hints), "You know that sermon was for you, right?" is not loving well.

This sacred conversation should allow you both to hear what stood out most, and result in you *getting* one another in a more meaningful way.

Sacred Time: Prayer

One of the most intimate, powerful conversations you can have with your spouse is in a collective conversation with God — in other words, praying together. Most couples find praying together to be awkward and uncomfortable. Seeing it as a vulnerable time of sharing our innermost thoughts, we become preoccupied with the idea that someone is listening and worry too much that the words are "right" and make sense. Like anything that is awkward at first, it takes time and practice for praying aloud with your spouse to become comfortable.

If you have never prayed with your spouse, here are a few ways to begin:

- **Ask your spouse, "What can I pray for you today?"** It is powerful to know your spouse is praying for you — whether for a specific conversation, a specific meeting, or a challenge you are facing. In knowing these important details, you are collectively growing with God in carrying each other's burdens.

- **Use PRAY.** This "prayer formula" may take away some of the anxiety from prayer. You could also write out your prayers and exchange pages with your spouse, asking him or her to pray for what you have written.

  - **P:** Praise — Praise God specifically for His character, His creation and His presence in your life
  - **R:** Repent — Confess to God your shortcomings and turn from your sin
  - **A:** Appreciation — Express appreciation for the gifts God has given you
  - **Y:** Your needs — Express your need for help from God

- **Offer a nighttime prayer.** If you have younger kids, start at bedtime and ask each person — husband, wife and child — to thank God for three things aloud in prayer. This simple prayer not only teaches your child a wonderful spiritual discipline, but it develops the discipline for you as a couple.

  If you don't have children, you may also want to try a nighttime prayer by taking turns expressing thanks before going to sleep. Prayers of thanksgiving are refreshing and a wonderful way to connect with the Lord.

The Sacred Prayer Conversation

If you feel overwhelmed when you first try this sacred conversation, start small. If one partner is reluctant to pray aloud, suggest that he or she simply conclude the prayer with "In Christ's name we pray, Amen."

The hardest part will be getting started. Not unlike most things that intimidate us, the anticipation is often bigger than the event. Prayer by prayer, you'll find that this sacred time opens up a new and meaningful way to grow in *getting* your spouse.

Sacred Time: Study

If you are the only one in your marriage in a Bible study, you know how things can get "lost in translation" when you try to tell your spouse something you learned in class. Studying the Bible *together* allows you to experience the impact of Scripture as a team.

How to develop the spiritual discipline of Study:

- **Devotional reading.** Devotionals are a short, daily reading based on Scripture. Choose a devotional and read it daily, then share for five minutes what the devotional means to you. You could share one book and take turns writing your thoughts about the devotional somewhere on the page. This is an easy way to read together and share ideas by reflecting your impressions in writing.

- **At-home Bible Study.** Pick a book of the Bible you want to study and choose an accompanying study guide you can use together. Your local Christian bookstore will have several easy-to-use study guides. Then set a weekly time to discuss the lesson together.

- **Small-group participation.** Determine if your church offers small groups that allow you and your spouse to study and fellowship with other married couples. Often, an easy way to begin studying the Bible together is to do so with others.

The Sacred Study Conversation

Within your Bible Study discussions, you will begin a rich understanding of where your spouse is both personally and spiritually. Perhaps one of the best questions you can ask your spouse as you examine Scripture is, "What is God saying to you in this verse (or passage)?"

Seek to understand and honor one another's answers — never judge or condemn.

Sacred Time: Confession

If you are like most, this is the spiritual discipline that makes you cringe! Who *wants* to admit when you've been wrong or share when you've been weak? But expressing this kind of vulnerability before the Lord and others opens the opportunity to grow stronger in God.

Consider these two types of confession:

- **Use the Forgiveness Formula.** When you have wronged your spouse, remember this:

    - Confess what you did wrong, specifically. *("I am sorry I was 30 minutes late.")*

    - Make amends by asking for forgiveness. *("Will you please forgive me?)*

    - Repent by intentionally focusing on not replicating the behavior in the future. *("Next time, I am going to focus on estimating my travel time more accurately.")*

- **Confess spiritual challenges**. Tell your spouse what you struggle with in your walk with God. Share your struggle with anger, patience or specific unhealthy habits. This not only invites your spouse into that sacred space, but also gives your spouse a specific request for prayer.

The Sacred Confession Conversation

This sacred conversation may be the most challenging for you both. Sometimes your spouse's confession may not directly impact you, though at times it may cut you to your core. That's why this moment is sacred. When your spouse is sharing his or her shortcomings with you, and asking for your forgiveness, you have an opportunity to display the kind of love Christ displayed to you. (Remember, the New Commandment? *Love like Christ.*)

Whenever your spouse has the courage and boldness to confess his or her wrongdoing or spiritual challenge, hold their intimacy sacred. Do not use this confession as a weapon against your spouse at a later date. Rather, commit to your spouse that you will ask the Lord for His help with this challenge and how you can best show support to your spouse.

As difficult as it can be to share weaknesses and our wrongdoings with one another, it strengthens your marriage, and grows you significantly closer to God. If you can master this conversation, and love one another well through it, your marriage will find freedom in ways that it cannot when you keep the hidden parts to yourself.

Love Redefined

Our hope is that you would scrap your worldly definition of love for a new one. By putting God first, you will see that your worth and happiness does not come from your spouse, but from the One who created you. If your relationship priorities are ordered correctly, you both should reap great benefits from living out a biblical definition of love as you enjoy the sacred partnership that you share.

Please remember that this new understanding of love takes continual refocusing on your part. The world's definition of love will creep in far more often than the biblical definition. But, when you choose to remember your wedding vow "to love and to cherish" — now with God as #1 in your marriage — you should find that the biblical model of love profoundly transforms the way you love your spouse.

Remember the Goal

Remember the goal of Sacred Time is to *get* your spouse in the most meaningful way. Sacred Time conversations are the deepest you can go, especially if your goal is to hear, understand and know your spouse. You can know one another's week ahead schedule and have a plan for landscaping your backyard, but if you miss the opportunity to love your spouse with a biblical kind of love — you may never fully *get* your spouse. You may also always wonder what is missing. Open up your marriage to God's presence, the author of love, and the one who *gets* you most.

NEXT STEPS

As you begin considering what Sacred Time will look like for you as a couple, consider these next steps:

- Dedicate an Intentional Date Night to discuss The Love Triangle. What has been your historical definition of love? What do the four Scriptures presented in this chapter mean to each of you? How can you adopt the Scriptures into your marriage?

- Determine which of the spiritual disciplines and sacred conversations you want to commit to for the next 90 days. Discuss what it would look like if you were both committed to this discipline. Understand <u>why</u> this discipline is so important to you as a couple, so when you grow weary, it can serve as your motivation to move forward.

- If you do nothing else, pray together that God will spark a new interest in growing your relationship with Him. Ask God to show you the next steps of how to develop a regular Sacred Time in your week for your marriage.

REFLECTION QUESTIONS

1. What cultural references or standards of comparison have shaped your definition of love?

2. Ask your spouse what love looks like to him or her. Have your spouse give you specific examples of when he or she feels loved well by you.

3. Discuss ways in which you are exhibiting the Great Commandment in your life. Then share with your spouse the ways you see him or her living out the Great Commandment.

4. Considering the New Commandment, how can you and your spouse develop your relationship with God to love one another better?

5. Which of the disciplines presented would you like to commit to in your marriage?

Be the
Twenty Percent

by Gregg Medlyn

One of our main goals of writing *Getting Me* was to help you realize that you are not alone. Many of the issues you and your spouse are dealing with are very similar to those of people all around you. However, what ultimately separates your marriage from every other marriage is what *you* choose to do with *yours*.

In fact, the marital issues presented in this book are so common, that it brings marriages just like yours into my office seeking help every week. As a solution-focused therapist, I help couples find ways to solve the problem or pain that brings them in. I also want you to begin visualizing what you want your marriage to look like. Regardless of whether it has lost its steam —

> *One of our main goals of writing **Getting Me** was to help you realize that you are not alone.*

or is contemplating a separation — there is still time to make your marriage one that brings about connection and fulfillment for you both.

I tell every couple that comes to me for help, that they have three choices.

1. They can fix their marriage.

2. They can end their marriage.

3. They can do nothing — and continue doing what they have been doing. (Albert Einstein defined this as insanity!)

Our hope is that you and your spouse will choose option 1. Regardless of what led you to purchase *Getting Me*, our desire is that you will be part of the twenty percent of couples that are courageous and disciplined enough to do the hard work of strengthening their marriages. Reading *Getting Me* together with your spouse is a great first step in the journey toward enriching your marriage.

Whether or not *you* believe it, Candace and I wholeheartedly believe there is hope available for your marriage. But, the outcome you desire has to be *your* decision, and you must stay committed to doing the work required — day in and day out — to experience that outcome. We can't want something more for your marriage than you want for your marriage. With every *Getting Me* conversation, you have to make the choice to hear, understand and know your spouse so that he or she feels loved, appreciated, and respected. It's hard work, but the reward is unlike no other.

Can People Really Change?

I'm often asked whether or not I believe people can change. I do. But the truth is, change is hard. However, if you value something enough, you will sacrifice and work hard for it.

Change is especially hard work for couples where trust has been broken, the relationship has been damaged, or when you have resolved to the belief that your spouse will never *get* you. You may have struggled with this as you read through *Getting Me*.

This is why marriage therapy is essential to change. Seeking the help of a professional can help provide a strategic plan to help a person to grow. For every person that seeks professional help, there are three phases of effective therapy.

1. Stop the pain

2. Heal

3. Grow — the only phase where real, lasting transformation occurs

As I mentioned, most of my clients come see me when their marital pain is too much to bear. A couple comes hoping I can help stop the pain. Once we can get to the place where the pain has stopped, it's essential we move to the next phase of healing before one can actually start to see real growth. Then and only then can you see a truly changed person or truly changed marriage.

Sadly, the vast majority of people stop therapy when the pain has stopped, but before they've healed and grown. For instance, in a marriage where a couple divorces, one might find the marital pain that brought him and his wife to therapy stops immediately when the separation occurs. Instead of continuing to seek help for healing, one might use this pain-free time to stop therapy and start dating again. Rationalizing it with, "Why go to therapy anymore if the pain is gone?" Wrong mentality.

 I always urge my clients not to date anyone who hasn't been divorced for more than two years. Any time less than that, and a person has not allowed himself enough time to

heal. For a person to really change, he must heal first to allow room to grow. This is one reason second marriages have a 50 percent higher divorce rate than first marriages, because we tend to change spouses without changing ourselves. It's also the reason why most couples have the same fight over and over. (Refer to our videocast: "Emotional Equivalence in Marriage" for more.)

Only a small percentage of people actually grow or change. But it is possible.

Remove Blame, Start Healing the Pain

Couples experience vastly different kinds of pain in their marriages. In the past few weeks alone, couples have come to me because of pain from:

- The loss of a child, a parent, a job

- Making bad financial decisions — typically overspending or insufficient budgeting

- A partner having an affair

- A partner having an addiction — most commonly alcohol, drugs or pornography

- Sexual issues — typically lack of sex or one partner wanting something the other partner refuses to do

- Abuse — typically verbal and emotional

- Empty nest issues or retirement issues

- Diagnosis of a mental or physical disorder — typically depression or cancer

Regardless the issue, struggling couples always feel disconnected. They don't get along as well as they did in the past, they fight more, spend less time together, or are disappointed with their partner or their marriage.

At the point in which they sit down across from me, their blame-game is at an all-time high. It's *always* their spouse's fault. Even in the case of extramarital affairs, I have seen the partner who had the affair blame their spouse for their "having to have" the affair. In this case, I acknowledge the person who had the affair is 100 percent at fault for having the affair. But, I always remind couples they are both equally responsible for the state of their marriage.

We cannot blame our partners for our choices. There is no hope of "fixing" your marriage, or healing your pain, until each person takes responsibility for his or her own issues, part, and actions. I want every couple to understand that each person plays a part in both the healthiness and unhealthiness of their relationship. Only when each partner can say, "I am the problem," can we move beyond blame and can look for solutions. (See our videocast: "When Your Spouse Won't Take Responsibility" for more.)

> *There is no hope of "fixing" your marriage, or healing your pain, until each person takes responsibility for his or her own issues, part, and actions.*

This is difficult for most couples. I rarely have an individual take ownership for their part of the problem at our initial session. *"It's their fault!"*, I always hear. *"How could I be the problem?"* Blaming one another must be removed from the equation. Healing can't begin if it is always the other person's fault.

Taking Responsibility for the Hope of Resolution

Taking responsibility and being held accountable for your actions is very powerful in relationships, especially in relationships that hope to heal.

The hardest part of marriage therapy is the process of repenting or changing. I address the process of taking responsibility in all relations from a biblical viewpoint. I acknowledge these three scriptures to support what I believe is imperative to finding resolution.

1. Confess your sin to one another (James 5:16) — "I did this _____."

2. Make amends (2 Cor. 13:11) — "I am sorry and I know I hurt you."

3. Repent (Jer. 18:11c) — "Here is what I am going to do to change."

Once, a client told me about a time she walked upstairs to find her husband looking at pornography. This triggered many fears in her, as well as for her husband. The husband, instead of blaming his wife for "their lack of sex that was making him do it," which I hear so often, confessed his addiction. He apologized and said he knew he was hurting her and offered to remove the computer from the house, or into a more public space in the kitchen. We carefully worked through this process to help them make amends, and as difficult as it was for his wife to forgive him, she did. She then held him responsible for finding a support group to join.

Apply this scenario to any topic you may have in your marriage — from "harmless" white lies to alcohol addictions. It's important you take responsibility for your shortcomings and create accountability for change.

Some people will try to shorten this process by going straight to the "I'm sorry." But that leaves a significant part of the process out. Sorry *for what*? It's important that you take full responsibility for your actions — don't try to cut it short. The process of finding true resolution is always a three-step process: confess, make amends, and repent.

 Please note: Accepting responsibility and removing blame are especially difficult when there are major relationship issues like abuse, adultery, addiction, and mental illness. If any of these issues are present in your marriage, you must address these issues first. We highly recommend you seek the help of a professional and have referral sources listed at www.getting-me.com.

You may find the hardest part of confession is forgiving yourself. Ephesians 4:32 urges you and your spouse to be kind and compassionate to one another — to forgive one another, just as God through Christ has forgiven you. We hope you will apply this grace and mercy not only to one another, but also to yourself.

A Lifetime of *Getting* Your Spouse

When Candace and I started writing this book, we shared a common purpose: to help you and your spouse get involved in intentional, ongoing conversations that would create intimacy. We knew that the more you felt your spouse *gets* you, the more heard, understood and known you would feel.

I remind couples all throughout therapy that love is doing something — not always because you want to — but because it is important to your spouse.

You do it without resentment or complaining.

You do it with no expectation of anything in return.

You do it even when the other person doesn't deserve it.

Therefore, to fully solve any marital issue, you must listen to and seek to understand each other, while always showing love, appreciation, and respect. The more you hear, understand and know your spouse, the more your spouse will see and know you *get* him or her. This is not a one-time event, nor can it rely solely on your personal desire to engage. There will be times that you partake in *Getting Me* conversations because it's important to your spouse — which means that it's important for your marriage.

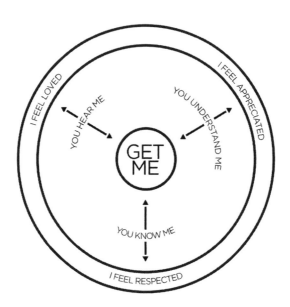

Before You Draw Your Final Conclusion

As your reading comes to a close, we urge you not to draw your final conclusion just yet. In fact, please don't draw any conclusions about *Getting Me* until you complete the following:

- **Read *Getting Me* more than once.** Unlike a typical novel, *Getting Me* should have connected with you on many different marital levels. Whether on the topic of intimacy, or how to approach conflict, or how to confess a shortcoming, it will benefit you greatly to read the material over together again. And then again.

- **Try each *Getting Me* conversation more than once**. Your first time engaging in a conversation should be considered a warm up, then consider the second attempt a refiner, and then consider every conversation after that an opportunity. Having one Intentional Date Night, or State of the Union conversation, or evening of praying together before bed will not make a lasting difference in your marriage. The conversations must remain ongoing, just as is the lifelong process of *getting* your spouse.

- **Commit to the Reflection Questions and Next Steps.** If you read through this book and skipped answering the questions or taking the next steps, we recommend that if you do nothing else, you commit to this purposeful portion of the book. These sections are critical to helping you engage with the content of the chapter.

Be the Twenty Percent

It will take time to get good at *getting* your spouse. We know. Candace and I have been implementing these same six *Getting Me* conversations into our own marriages, and it is hard work. We don't get it right every time (Ruth and John can attest!), but we keep trying. *Getting* your spouse is a lifelong process — one that requires intentionality and ongoing commitment.

Our prayer is that you will not only choose to do the hard work, but will also choose to be the twenty percent who proves that the selfless pursuit of *getting* your spouse is completely worth it.